KREM 2

In the Kitchen

In the Kitchen

LAURA PAPETTI
Writer/Editor

TAMARA MCGREGOR
Copy Editor & Marketing

BARBARA GRANT
Project Coordinator

CARY SEWARD
Promotions

DAWN ROBERSON
Cover & Logo Designer

ALAN BISSON
Cover Photograph

LISA MATHEWS
Lawton Printing

COREY HOGAN BIPPES
Layout & Design

ISBN: 1-890225-06-1

We were overwhelmed by the amazing support our viewers provided.
Unfortunately, we were unable to kitchen test all the recipes.

KREM-TV
4103 South Regal Street, Spokane, WA 99223
(509) 448-2000 • www.krem.com

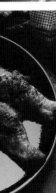
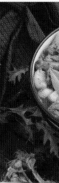

KREM CHANNEL 2

50 years. I guess time really does fly when you're having fun.

What an amazing journey we have all traveled together over the airwaves. On October 29th, 1954, KREM Television flipped the switch and said "hello" to the Inland Northwest. It has been a grand adventure, and through it all we have both witnessed and told many stories. Think back for a moment and remember some of the extraordinary events over the past five decades. Events like the World's Fair, presidential visits, Ice Storm and Fire Storm just to name a few. There were joyous occasions we celebrated together and sad times that united us in sorrow.

Through it all, we could always count on you, our viewers. You've allowed us into your homes each night. You've made us part of your daily lives, and in a sense, part of your family. And for that we are so very thankful. We are also especially thankful for the stories you've helped us tell through the years. Because, after all, news is about people, so our stories were about you.

Once again, we relied on your help when putting together this charity cookbook. And of course, as always, you came through. We received hundreds of recipes, many of them longtime family favorites. Unfortunately, we could not use them all, there were just too many. So if your recipe is not in this book, we apologize, and ask for your understanding.

We decided to print this cookbook in conjunction with our Golden Anniversary because we thought "what better way to celebrate 50 years than with food". The kitchen is often the hub of the family and with that in mind, we ask only one thing. When you make one of these recipes, remember to raise your glass in a toast and know that you are part of a vibrant community and an important part of the KREM family.

Thank you for 50 wonderful years.

From our kitchen to yours-Bon Appetit.

Upper left: Thank goodness the cameras got lighter. **Upper middle:** *Taking a closer look at local issues—Telescope 1970.* **Upper right:** *The year was 1966 and KREM was on the scene of big events.* **Center left:** *Crewcuts are gone (well-mostly) but KREM is here to stay.* **Center:** *We still drive American cars but nothing this sporty. News has always moved fast.* **Center right:** *We go above the rest to get the story.* **Lower left:** *Looking back we were always forecasting ahead. Long gone are the stick-on numbers. Now all the weather maps are computer generated.* **Lower middle:** *Showcasing the Inland Northwest.* **Lower right:** *Rick Aguilar (better known as Aggie) came to KREM in 1974. His hair has changed but he's still the greatest guy.*

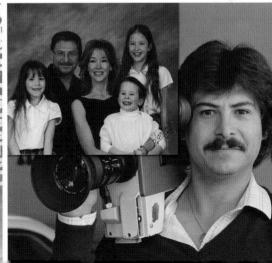

Breakfast

Blueberry Breakfast Treats

INGREDIENTS:	
⅓	cup butter
2	cups flour
2	tsp. baking powder
¼	tsp. salt
1	cup sugar
¾	cup milk
1	egg
1	cup blueberries

1 Preheat oven to 350°.

2 Stir shortening to soften. To shortening add sifted flour, baking powder, salt, and sugar. Add milk and beat for 2 minutes. Add egg. Beat for 1 minute. Fold in blueberries. Pour into greased 8 x 8 x 2 inch pan. Bake for 50 minutes. ∾

—*Recipe submitted by Daryl Romeyn.*

This recipe is from our favorite morning weather guy, Daryl Romeyn. Being the outdoorsy-type he likes to whip up a quick (and filling) breakfast before leaving the house for one of his adventures.

Daryl grew up in Detroit. After graduating from the University of Michigan he jumped in his truck and headed west to pursue his true love - exploring the wild mountain backcountry. Daryl has been in Spokane for 17 years. When out in the wild-the weatherman turned explorer-travels with donkeys (they carry the gear!). When he's not in the yard (he grows his own cherries and asparagus) or at work forecasting the weather on KREM 2 he's up in the hills. On your next hike look for the guy with three donkeys following him and ask for a weather update.

Savory Eggs

INGREDIENTS:	
2	cups American cheese, grated
¼	cup butter
1	cup light cream
½	tsp. salt
¼	tsp. pepper
2	tsp. prepared mustard
12	eggs, slightly beaten

1 Preheat oven to 325°.

2 Spread cheese into a greased 13 x 9 pan. Dot with butter. In a separate bowl, mix cream, salt, pepper, and mustard. Pour half of this mixture over the cheese. Pour beaten eggs into baking dish. Add remaining cream mixture. Bake for 40 minutes. ❧

—Linda Fisher sent us this recipe from Colfax, WA. This recipe is not for those watching their weight. It's for those who love a good breakfast.

Dee's Casserole

INGREDIENTS:	
1	lb. pork sausage
6	eggs
2	cups milk
1	tsp. salt
1	tsp. ground mustard
6	slices white bread, cubed
1	cup cheddar cheese, shredded

The night before: In a skillet, brown and crumble sausage. Drain and set aside. In a large bowl, beat eggs. Add milk, salt, and mustard to eggs. Stir in bread cubes, cheese, and sausage. Pour mixture into greased 11 x 7 baking dish. Cover and refrigerate overnight.

The next morning: Remove from refrigerator about 30 minutes before baking. Bake, uncovered for 40 minutes at 350° or until knife inserted near center comes out clean. ❧

—This recipe was sent in by Dee Smith.

Asparagus Eggs

Rose Pohito from Wenatchee, WA, sent in this easy scrambled egg dish.

§ She boils a handful of asparagus stalks for a few minutes, until slightly tender. She then puts them in a frying pan and cooks for a few more minutes. She adds 2 beaten eggs and cooks until done. Delicious combo! ❧

Quick Fix

Breakfast Casserole

INGREDIENTS:
4 eggs
2⅓ cups milk
1 can cream of mushroom soup
¾ tsp. dry mustard
1 to 1½ lbs. country sausage
½ cup onion, chopped
5 mushrooms, sliced
½ cup walnuts, chopped
12 slices white bread, cubed with crusts removed
¾ lb. cheddar cheese
Non-stick spray

1 *Night before:* Spray a large baking dish with non-stick spray. Pour in enough milk to cover bottom of pan. Set aside baking dish.

2 In a separate bowl, combine eggs, remaining milk, soup, and mustard. In a skillet, brown sausage with onion and mushrooms. In the baking dish, put a layer of half the cubed bread, sausage mixture, walnuts, cheese, and milk mixture. Repeat layers one more time. Cover and refrigerate overnight.

Next morning: Preheat oven to 300°. Bake for 1 hour. ❧

—Linda Jones makes this for her children and grandchildren on Christmas morning. It's part of her family's tradition. Maybe it can be part of yours.

Breakfast Souffle

INGREDIENTS:
1 lb. cooked crab (or sausage)
6 slices of bread, cubed with crusts removed
1 cup sharp cheddar, grated
4 eggs
½ tsp. salt
½ tsp. dry mustard
2 cups milk

The night before: In a buttered 11 x 7 baking pan, layer bread cubes, crab, and cheese. Repeat layers until ingredients are used. In a separate bowl, beat eggs. Add salt, dry mustard, and milk to eggs. Pour egg mixture over the ingredients in the baking pan. Cover and refrigerate overnight.

The next morning: Preheat oven to 325°. Bake souffle about 45 minutes. Cover with foil if cheese is melting too fast. Serve with the following sauce if desired:

Sherry Mushroom Sauce:
1 10½ oz. can of cream of mushroom soup
¼ cup sherry
1 2 oz. can of mushroom pieces, drained

In a saucepan, blend soup, mushrooms, and sherry over low heat. Serve with breakfast souffle recipe. ❧

—Jean Nelson of Medical Lake, WA, adds crab to her breakfast souffle. Brunch anyone?

Stuffed French Toast

	INGREDIENTS:
8	large slices of bread, cubed
12	eggs
2	cups milk
⅓	cup maple syrup
1	8 oz. pkg. cream cheese
1	cup cooked bacon or sausage (optional)

Night before: Put half of the bread cubes in a buttered 13 x 9 pan. Cut cream cheese into chunks and put it on top of the bread. If desired, add meat. Add the remaining bread cubes to baking dish. In a separate bowl, combine eggs, milk, and syrup. Beat well. Pour liquid over ingredients in baking dish. Cover and refrigerate overnight.

Next morning: Preheat oven to 325°. Bake for 1 hour at 325°. ∾

—This is a very special recipe sent in by Bonnie Wordell. Her mother passed away from breast cancer. She says her mom was a fantastic cook and left behind a handwritten cookbook of her own recipes. We are honored to include one in our book.

B&B Style French Toast

	INGREDIENTS:
½	cup flour
½	Tbsp. baking powder
¾	cup milk
½	tsp. vanilla
½	Tbsp. cinnamon
1	egg
1	egg white
1½	Tbsp. sugar
⅛	cup oil
4-6	slices of bread

1 In a bowl, beat eggs. Add sugar, oil, cinnamon, milk, and vanilla. Mix well. Add flour and baking powder. Dip bread into egg mixture.

2 Cook over medium heat until slightly golden on each side of bread. Top with your favorite syrup or fruit! ∾

—This recipe is from Kirsten Russell here at KREM 2 News. She is quite the cook! You can refrigerate the finished product and toast a piece at a time if you want. Perfect for those rushed mornings.

Blueberry French Toast

INGREDIENTS:

Toast:

12	slices day old bread, cubed with crusts removed
12	eggs
2	8 oz. pkgs. cream cheese
1	cup fresh or frozen blueberries
2	cups milk
⅓	cup honey or maple syrup

Sauce:

1	cup sugar
1	cup fresh or frozen blueberries
2	Tbsp. corn starch
1	Tbsp. butter
1	cup water

Night before:

1 Put half of the bread cubes in a greased 13 x 9 baking dish. Cut cream cheese into cubes and place over bread. Top cream cheese with the other half of bread cubes.

2 In a bowl, beat eggs. Add milk and honey or syrup. Mix well. Pour mixture over bread cubes. Cover and refrigerate overnight.

Next morning:

1 Preheat oven to 350°.

2 Cook for 25-30 minutes.

3 Meanwhile, combine sugar and cornstarch in a saucepan. Add water. Bring mixture to a boil over medium heat. Boil for 3 minutes while stirring constantly. Stir in blueberries. Reduce heat and simmer about 8 minutes. Remove from heat and stir in butter. Serve over toast. ∾

—This recipe was sent in by Alice Schofield. Perfect for blueberry season (or huckleberries!).

Pigs in the Orchard

Quick Fix

Lonnie Demaray sent us this recipe from her Spokane kitchen.

⑧ Lonnie takes a large, heavy skillet and puts in 8 lean link sausages. She peels and slices 3 or 4 apples and adds it to the pan. Then, add just enough water to cover the sausages. Cover and cook on medium high heat until the apples look transparent. Remove cover, turn down heat to medium and continue to cook. Watch the sausage and apples careful as to not burn. Turn sausages to brown on all sides and cook until apples are a caramel brown. ∾

Avocado & Goat Cheese Breakfast Muffin

This is the perfect brunch food and all it takes is a few minutes and a toaster. Don Gauld sent us this easy recipe. Don toasts and butters an English muffin. On the bottom half, he places a think layer of goat cheese or cream cheese. He tops that with a slice of avocado and heaps on a layer of sprouts. He tops his creation with a twist of lemon and then tops with the other half of muffin. ∽

Light as a Feather Waffles

INGREDIENTS:	
2	cups waffle mix
1	egg
½	cup vegetable oil
1⅓	cups club soda

1 In a bowl, combine all ingredients until well blended.

2 Pour batter onto hot waffle iron and cook until golden. You can cook the waffles and refrigerate the leftovers. Pop one in the toaster before you leave for work or school. ∽

—If you are serious about a good waffle then try this recipe sent in by Dolly Patterson. She cooks them up in her Spokane kitchen.

Oatmeal Pancakes

INGREDIENTS:	
1	cup oats
1	cup whole wheat flour
¼	cup dry non-fat milk
1	tsp. baking soda
½	cup wheat germ
½	tsp. salt
1	Tbsp. brown sugar
1	egg, beaten
1	cup buttermilk
¼	cup butter or margarine, melted

1 In a large bowl, combine all the dry ingredients. Stir in egg, buttermilk, and butter. Drop about a 1/4 cup of mixture onto a hot griddle and cook until golden on each side. Serve with maple syrup if desired. ∽

—Linda Jones from Chewelah, WA, sent us this recipe for oatmeal pancakes. A perfect warm breakfast for a cold winter day.

Russian Tea

INGREDIENTS:	
1¾	cup Tang (dry)
1	large pkg. lemonade mix (dry)
¾	cup instant tea (dry)
1½	cup sugar
1	tsp. cinnamon
½	tsp. ground cloves

Mix all ingredients together. Keep in a sealed container. Use two teaspoons of mixture in a cup of boiling water. Sip slowly and enjoy the morning. ❧

—Need something warm to drink to go with your breakfast on a cold morning? Here's a recipe from Mary Arnold of Coeur d'Alene, ID.

Granola Cereal

INGREDIENTS:	
4	cups oatmeal
½	cup flaked coconut
¼	cup sunflower seeds, shelled
½	tsp. salt
½	cup honey
½	cup wheat germ
1	tsp. cinnamon
⅓	cup vegetable oil
1	cup raisins
1	cup dates, finely chopped

1 Preheat oven to 300°.

2 In a large bowl, mix all ingredients except for the raisins and dates. Spread mixture onto a jelly roll pan. Cook in oven for about 30 minutes or until mixture is a light brown. Stir about every 7 minutes. Remove from oven and add raisins and dates. Mix well and cool. Store in a plastic bag in a cool place. ❧

—Kathy and Roger Premo make this creation. It's perfect for a healthy breakfast.

Banana-Apple Breakfast Bars

INGREDIENTS:

Bars:

2	Tbsp. honey
1	Tbsp. maple syrup
6	Tbsp. canola oil
1	cup flour
1	tsp. cinnamon, divided
¼	tsp. salt
½	tsp. ground nutmeg
½	cup slivered almonds, coarsely chopped
1	cup oats

Topping:

2	ripe bananas, mashed
2	eggs
¼	tsp. ground ginger
1	tsp. cinnamon
3	Tbsp. honey
½	cup apples, finely chopped

1 Preheat oven to 375°.

2 To make the bars: mix honey, maple syrup, and canola oil.

3 In a separate bowl; combine flour, cinnamon, salt, nutmeg, and chopped almonds. Add honey mixture. Stir in oats.

4 Press bar mixture into greased 9x13 pan. Bake for approximately 15 minutes. Remove from oven.

5 Meanwhile; blend together bananas, eggs, ginger, cinnamon, and honey. Spread over baked bar mixture. Sprinkle with chopped apples. Bake for 15 minutes or until done in the center. Let cool and cut into bars. ✎

—This recipe was submitted by KREM 2's Drashell Schmidt. When Drashell isn't working, she's often running. This recipe gives her some energy to get a jump on the competition.

Morning Chocolate Surprise

Take 2 sheets of puff pastry (from the frozen food section) and thaw. Cut into 12 squares. In the middle of each square place about 3½ oz. of chocolate. You can use squares of chocolate or a couple tablespoons of chocolate chips. Wrap the pastry around the chocolate. Place fold side down on baking sheet covered in parchment paper. Top the pastries with an egg glaze. Bake at 400° degrees for about 15 minutes. Serve warm. ✎

Breads

Nana's Banana Bread

INGREDIENTS:	
1½	cups very ripe bananas, mashed
1	egg
1	cup sugar
1½	cup flour
1	tsp. salt
1	tsp. baking soda
¾	cup walnuts, chopped (optional)
⅔	cup chocolate chips, (optional, but good)

1 Preheat oven to 350°.

2 In large bowl, combine banana and egg. Sift together dry ingredients. Add to banana mixture and stir. Add optional ingredients if desired.

3 Pour into a greased and floured bread pan. Bake for 15 minutes at 350°. Lower temperature to 325°. Bake 1 more hour. ❧

—*This recipe is submitted by Dawn and Sean in loving memory of Sean's grandmother, Nana Tarte.*

▲ *When Dawn Picken is not reporting for 2 On Your Side or co-anchoring the First Edition, she runs marathons for fun. Yea. Marathons for fun. The woman is a machine.*

◀ *Besides being an award winning journalist, Dawn has also taught public speaking at EWU. Though she's busy, she always makes time for her husband, Sean Stanelun and their sweet baby girl, Fiona.*

Crites Coffee Cake

INGREDIENTS:	
1	cup sugar
1	cup brown sugar
1	cup butter
3	cups flour
½	cup nuts, chopped
2	tsp. cinnamon
1	cup buttermilk
2	large eggs
1½	tsp. vanilla
½	tsp. salt
1	tsp. baking soda
1	tsp. baking powder

1 Preheat oven to 350°.

2 In a medium bowl; combine sugar, brown sugar, butter, flour, nuts, and cinnamon until crumbly. Set aside 1 cup of crumb mixture for topping. To remaining mixture, add buttermilk, eggs, vanilla, salt, baking powder, and baking soda. Mix by hand to a lumpy consistency.

3 Pour into greased 13 x 9 pan. Level smooth and top with reserved crumb mixture. Bake for 35-40 minutes. Toothpick should come out clean when done. Serve warm. ∾

—Recipe submitted by Nicole Crites.

▲ *Nicole Crites is like everybody's sister. She's sweet, smart, and funny. Nicole hails from Tucson, Arizona, (where she has a huge family) but now she's a true Northwest gal.*

▶ *Nicole and her husband Dave have settled into the Spokane area. When she's not brightening up the First Edition or tracking down a breaking story, Nicole loves to quilt and paint. Her patriotic quilt inspired by 9/11 is stunning! Nicole has a smile as sweet as the coffee cake she sneaks into the newsroom for the morning crew.*

Amish Friendship Bread

INGREDIENTS:	
1	cup vegetable oil
1½	cups sugar
1	tsp. vanilla
3	large eggs
½	tsp. salt
2	tsp. cinnamon
2½	cups flour
1¼	cups milk
½	tsp. baking soda
1	3.4 oz. pkg. instant vanilla pudding
1½	tsp. baking powder
⅓	cup black walnuts (optional)
	Cinnamon & Sugar

1 Preheat oven to 325°.

2 In a large bowl; combine oil, sugar, vanilla, eggs, salt, and cinnamon. Add flour, milk, baking soda, pudding, baking powder, and walnuts (if desired). Mix well.

3 Grease 2 large loaf pans and sprinkle with a mixture of cinnamon and sugar. Pour batter into pans. Bake for 1 hour. Drizzle with glaze if desired. ❧

—This recipe was sent in by Mary Helgerson of Bonners Ferry, ID. Make it for a friend today!

Swedish Flat Bread

INGREDIENTS:	
2¾	cups unsifted flour
¼	cup sugar
½	tsp. baking soda
½	tsp. salt
½	cup butter
1	cup buttermilk

1 Preheat oven to 400°.

2 In a large bowl; mix flour, sugar, baking soda, and salt. Cut in the butter then add buttermilk. Mix well.

3 Shape into a ball. Break off 1-inch ball shaped pieces. Roll into thin rounds about 4-5 inches in diameter.

4 Place on ungreased baking sheets. Bake for 5 minutes. Watch closely as to not burn! ❧

—From Worley, ID, comes this recipe for Swedish flat bread. It's from the kitchen of Vivian Sneve.

Monkey Bread

INGREDIENTS:	
Bread:	
4	cans biscuits
¾	cup sugar
1	tsp. cinnamon
Glaze:	
1	cup of sugar
¾	cup margarine
1 ½	tsp. cinnamon

1 Preheat oven to 350°.

2 Mix sugar and cinnamon together. Cut biscuits into quarters and toss into the sugar mixture. Place sugar-coated dough into a greased tube or bundt pan. In a saucepan, mix glaze ingredients. Bring to a boil. Pour glaze mixture over biscuits. Bake for 20-25 minutes. Serve warm! ∽

—This recipe comes from Lisa Carper in Oroville, WA. She says it's a favorite in her after-school cooking class.

Applesauce Spice Bread

INGREDIENTS:	
2	cups flour
1	tsp. baking soda
1	tsp. cinnamon
½	tsp. nutmeg
¼	tsp. cloves
½	cup vegetable oil
1¾	cup sugar
3	eggs
1 ½	cups applesauce

1 Preheat oven to 325°.

2 In a large bowl; sift together flour, baking soda, cinnamon, nutmeg, and cloves. In a small bowl, mix oil, sugar, eggs, and applesauce. Pour oil mixture into dry ingredients. Mix for 2 minutes at medium speed. Pour batter into 2 small greased loaf pans. Bake for 50 minutes. ∽

—Rosie Loveland from Othello, WA, sent us this recipe. Perfect comfort food on a cold day!

Applesauce Bread

INGREDIENTS:	
½	cup shortening
¾	cup sugar
2	eggs
1	tsp. vanilla
2	cups sifted flour
1	tsp. baking powder
1	tsp. baking soda
1	tsp. salt
1	tsp. cinnamon
½	tsp. nutmeg
1	cup applesauce
½	cup raisins
½	cup walnuts

1 Preheat oven to 350°

2 In a bowl; cream shortening, sugar, eggs, and vanilla. Add flour, baking powder, baking soda, salt, cinnamon, and nutmeg. Stir in applesauce, raisins, and nuts.

3 Bake for 1 hour at 350° or until toothpick comes out clean. ∾

—*This comes from the kitchen of Shirley Borns in Hayden, ID.*

Boston Brown Bread

INGREDIENTS:	
1	cup rye flour
1	cup whole wheat flour
1	cup corn meal
1	tsp. salt
2	tsp. baking soda
2	cups buttermilk
¾	cup molasses

1 In a large bowl; combine all the ingredients. Mix thoroughly. Pour batter into greased tin cans of various sizes. ***Twila recommends saving empty spaghetti sauce or pumpkin cans to steam bread.***

2 Cover each container with wax paper and hold in place with a rubber band.

3 Place on rack in large covered pot and steam for 3 hours. Cool on rack and slide from can to cool thoroughly. ∾

—*This recipe comes from the kitchen of Twila Little. She cooks up this bread in her Coeur d'Alene kitchen.*

Nina's Camping Bread

INGREDIENTS:	
2½	cups water
2	cups raisins
4	tsp. baking soda
2	cups brown sugar
3	Tbsp. oil or melted shortening
1	tsp. salt
4	cups unbleached flour
1	cup broken nutmeats (shelled nuts)

Night before: Bring water to a boil and pour over raisins and baking soda. Let stand overnight or until very cool.

1 *Next day:* Preheat oven to 350°.

2 To the raising mixture add; brown sugar, oil, salt, flour, and nutmeats. Pour batter into 2 well greased bread pans. Bake for 1 hour and test with toothpick. ❧

—This recipe caught our eye not just because of the bread but the story that went with it. Nina Bauer of Spokane writes, "This is a wonderful bread my husband and I took with us when we went camping, trailriding, or had parties at home. I received this recipe from a friend who was in her 70's and that was 32 years ago. They always took this bread on their trips also. I am 87-years-old now and my husband is gone but memories last forever. Yours Truly, Nina L. Bauer." Thank you Nina. Now we can share your memories and your recipe!

Jam Dandy Coffee Cake

INGREDIENTS:	
1½	cups flour
2½	tsp. baking powder
¼	cup shortening
¾	cup milk
¼	cup sugar
1	egg
¼	cup brown sugar
¼	cup chopped nuts
⅔	cup jam (flavor of choice)

1 Preheat oven to 375°.

2 In a large bowl; combine flour, baking powder, shortening, milk, sugar and egg. With quick strokes, beat 50 times with a fork.

3 Pour into a greased 9 x 9 square pan. Sprinkle with brown sugar and nuts. Dot with jam. Bake for 25-30 minutes. ❧

—This recipe is from Leah Goehner from Spokane. This and a cup of coffee, enough said.

Davenport Hotel Coffee Cake

INGREDIENTS:

Batter:

1	cup butter, softened
2	cups sugar
2	eggs
1	cup sour cream
½	tsp. vanilla
2	cups flour
1	tsp. baking powder
½	tsp. salt

Topping:

1	cup walnuts
2	tsp. cinnamon
2	tsp. brown sugar

1 Preheat oven to 350°.

2 In a bowl, cream butter and sugar with a mixer. Add eggs, sour cream, and vanilla. Gradually, add flour, baking powder, and salt. Mix until batter is smooth. Pour half the mixture into a greased 9-inch round cake pan.

3 In a separate bowl, combine walnuts, cinnamon, and brown sugar. Sprinkle half of the walnut mixture over batter in cake pan. Cover with remaining batter. Top with remaining walnut mixture. Bake for 1 hour. ❧

—This recipe (served at the Davenport) comes from the Worthy family.

Butter Crumshers Coffee Cake

INGREDIENTS:

Batter:

½	cup margarine
1	8 oz. pkg. cream cheese
1¼	cup sugar
2	eggs
1	tsp. vanilla
½	cup milk
2	cups sifted flour
2	tsp. baking powder
½	tsp. baking soda
½	tsp. salt

Topping:

¼	cup margarine (cold)
½	cup flour
½	cup brown sugar
½	cup nuts (optional)

Preheat oven to 350°. In a bowl; cream margarine, cream cheese, sugar, vanilla, and milk. Add eggs alternately with flour, baking powder, baking soda, and salt. End with dry ingredients. Blend well after each addition. Grease the bottom of a 9 x 13 baking dish. Pour in batter. In a separate bowl, combine cold margarine, flour, brown sugar, and nuts (if desired). Sprinkle on top of the cake batter. Bake for 30-40 minutes. ❧

—This recipe was sent in by Barb Teuton of Cheney, WA. She doesn't know what 'crumshers' means, but when it tastes this good it doesn't matter.

Cherry Almond Coffee Squares

INGREDIENTS:	
1	cup sour cream
¼	cup water
3	eggs
1	pkg. Betty Crocker Sour Cream Cake Mix
1	21 oz. can cherry pie filling
¼	cup almonds, sliced

1 Preheat oven to 350°.

2 Grease and flour 15½ x 10½ x 1 jelly roll pan. Meanwhile, mix together sour cream, water, and eggs. Stir in cake mix until moistened and slightly lumpy. Spread batter onto pan. Drop spoonfuls of pie filling every 3-4 inches apart onto batter. Bake for 25-30 minutes. Cook and sprinkle with almonds. ❧

—This recipe was sent in by Janet Wilkinson of Spokane.

Basic Dough Recipe

INGREDIENTS:	
1	cup milk (water can substitute)
⅓	cup shortening (oil can substitute)
½	cup sugar
1	Tbsp. salt
1	cup cold water
2	pkgs. yeast, dissolved in ½ cup warm water
2	eggs, beaten
10	cups flour

1 Preheat oven to 350°.

2 Together, boil milk, shortening, sugar, and salt. Cool to lukewarm. Meanwhile, dissolve yeast in ½ cup warm water. Combine milk mixture with yeast and eggs. Add flour one cup at a time. Knead until smooth and not sticky. Add flour as needed to achieve correct consistency. Bake for 20 minutes until slightly browned. ❧

—This is a recipe from Sue Parkert. It's a great basic dough recipe that you can use for everything from sweet rolls to dinner rolls.

Italian Spice Cheese Bread

Here's an easy way to dress up plain French bread. Slice a baguette or loaf of French bread lengthwise. In a small bowl, mix together a stick of butter with a small package of dry Italian dressing. Coat bread with butter mixture. Top with a cup of shredded mozzarella cheese. Broil for 2 minutes. Top with slices of tomato or roasted sundried tomatoes. Broil for one more minute. ❧

Quick Fix

Cinnamon Rolls

INGREDIENTS:

2½	cups warm water
2	pkgs. fast rising yeast
1	box yellow cake mix
6½	cups flour
3	eggs
½	cup oil
1	tsp. salt
1	tsp. vanilla
	Butter (room temperature)
	Brown sugar
	Cinnamon

1 Preheat oven to 350°.

2 In a bowl, combine warm water with yeast and cake mix. Mix for 3 minutes. Add 1 cup of flour. Stir in eggs, oil, salt, and vanilla. Beat until bubbles form. Add the rest of the flour 1 cup at a time. Soft dough should form. Knead dough for 5 minutes. Let rise until dough doubles. Roll out dough into a rectangle about ¼ inch thick. Spread with butter. Sprinkle on brown sugar and cinnamon. Roll up lengthwise. Spray 9 x 11 baking dish with non-stick spray. Slice dough into ½ inch thick pieces and place in baking pan. Let rise until doubled. Bake for 25 minutes. Add syrup or icing if desired. ∾

—This recipe is from LaVern Roberts. She cooks these up in her Omak, WA, kitchen.

Sour Cream Blueberry Muffins

INGREDIENTS:

Muffins:

1	7 oz. pkg. blueberry muffin mix
⅓	cup milk
¼	cup sour cream
3	tsp. raspberry jam

Glaze:

½	cup powdered sugar
2	tsp. milk
¼	tsp. almond extract

1 Preheat oven to 450°.

2 In medium bowl; combine muffin mix, milk, and sour cream. Stir until well blended. Spoon batter evenly into lined muffin cups. Spoon ½ tsp. jam into each muffin. Bake for 12-15 minutes, or until golden brown.

3 Meanwhile; in a small bowl, combine powdered sugar, milk, and almond extract. Stir until smooth. Remove muffins and cool for 2-3 minutes. Dip tops of warm muffins into glaze. ∾

—Jan Naugle from Spokane says this recipe has been in her family for years. Now it can be a family favorite for you.

Potato Rolls

INGREDIENTS:	
4½ to 5	cups flour
3	Tbsp. sugar
1½	tsp. salt
2	¼ oz. pkgs. yeast
3	Tbsp. butter or margarine
1¼	cup water
½	cup mashed potatoes
	Flour for kneading

1 Preheat oven to 350°.

2 In a bowl; combine 2-cups flour, sugar, yeast, and salt. In a saucepan, heat the water and butter together until lukewarm. Add to dry ingredients. Beat mixture until smooth. Stir in the potatoes. Slowly add remaining flour until a soft dough is formed.

3 Turn onto floured surface; knead until smooth and flexible. (about 6-8 minutes) Cover and let rise until it doubles in size. Punch down and form into desired shape.

4 Place in greased baking pans. Cover and let rise until dough doubles again (about 30 minutes). Bake for 12-15 minutes. Watch carefully and remove when golden brown. ❧

—This recipe was sent in by Dorothy Zimmerman from Deary, ID. She recommends serving these rolls with some of Tom Sherry's delicious barbecue.

Oatmeal Yeast Rolls

INGREDIENTS:	
2	pkgs. dry yeast
½	cup lukewarm water
⅓	cup milk, scalded
⅓	cup sugar
2	tsp. salt
½	cup margarine
1¼	cup oatmeal, uncooked
2	eggs, beaten
4½ to 5	cups flour

1 Preheat oven to 350°.

2 In a small bowl, soften yeast in lukewarm water. In a separate bowl, pour scalded milk over sugar, salt, and margarine. Cool until lukewarm. Stir in eggs and 1 cup of flour. Beat 100 strokes. Add softened yeast and oatmeal to mixture. Stir well. Stir in enough of the remaining flour to make a soft dough. Use extra flour if needed.

3 Round dough into a ball and place in a greased bowl. Cover and let rise in warm place until doubled in size. Punch down. Let dough rest for 10 minutes. Mold into desired shapes for dinner rolls. Cover and let double again. Bake for 20 minutes. ❧

—This recipe was sent in by Jim and Donna Cole.

Batter Buns

INGREDIENTS:	
⅔	cup warm water
1	pkg. dry yeast
2	Tbsp. sugar
¼	cup shortening
½	tsp. salt
1	egg
1⅔	cup flour

1 Preheat oven to 350°.

2 Dissolve yeast into warm water. Add sugar, shortening, salt, egg, and 1 cup flour. Mix well. Add remaining flour. Beat well.

3 Spoon batter into greased muffin tins filling them about half full. Let rise in warm place until batter reaches the top of the muffin tins. Bake for 18-20 minutes. ❧

—Bethi Stacy from Cusick, WA, sent us this recipe from her extensive recipe collection.

Orange-Cream Scones

INGREDIENTS:	
2	cups flour
1	Tbsp. baking powder
½	tsp. salt
¼	cup sugar
1	cup heavy cream
⅓	cup orange juice
1	Tbsp. grated orange peel
½	cup dried cranberries

1 Preheat oven to 425°.

2 In a bowl, combine flour, baking powder, salt and sugar. Stir until well mixed. Add cream and mix until dough holds together. Mix in orange peel and cranberries.

3 n a lightly floured surface, knead bread until dough loses most of its stickiness. Just knead about a ½ dozen times. Divide dough into 10-12 balls. Lightly flatten balls onto ungreased cookie sheet. Bake about 12 minutes. Tops should be golden. ❧

—This recipe is a favorite of Jessie Kane. Jessie is a KREM 2 producer and the resident animal lover. Jessie has two cute cats.

Broccoli Corn Bread

Betty Strickland likes to liven up her cornbread by adding a few different ingredients. She takes 2 8½ oz. pkgs. of corn muffin mix and adds the following: 4 beaten eggs, 1 small carton of small curd cottage cheese, 1 box of frozen broccoli (cooked and drained well), 1 cup of chopped onion, and 1½ sticks of melted margarine. She pours it into a greased 11 x 14 baking dish. She bakes her creation for 45 minutes at 350°. ∾

Pumpkin Bread

INGREDIENTS:	
2	cups sugar
4	eggs, beaten
1	cup margarine, melted
1	tsp. vanilla
1	small can pumpkin (not pie mix)
⅔	cup water
3½	cup flour
1½	tsp. baking soda
1	tsp. cinnamon
1	tsp. nutmeg
1	cup raisins
1	cup walnuts, chopped

Preheat oven to 350°. In a large bowl, mix together the first 6 ingredients. Add flour, baking soda, cinnamon, nutmeg, raisins, and walnuts. Pour into greased loaf pan (you can use 2 smaller ones if desired). Bake for 1 hour. (If using smaller pans bake for 30-40 minutes). ∾

—Nancy Morris sent us her award-winning pumpkin bread. She bakes it up in her Moscow, ID, kitchen.

Zucchini Bread

INGREDIENTS:	
3	eggs
2	cups sugar
1	cup vegetable oil
3	tsp. vanilla
2	cups zucchini, grated
3	cups flour
1	tsp. salt
1	tsp. baking soda
½	tsp. baking powder
4	tsp. cinnamon

1 Preheat oven to 350°.

2 In a bowl, mix eggs, sugar, oil, vanilla, and zucchini. Add the following: flour, salt, baking soda, baking powder, and cinnamon. Mix well. Pour batter into 2 greased and floured bread pans. Bake for 50-55 minutes. ∾

—This recipe was submitted by Tammy Anderson.

Appetizers

Sweet and Sour Meatballs

INGREDIENTS:	
1	jar concord grape jelly
1	jar chili sauce (red)
1	bag prepared frozen meatballs

Preheat oven to 350°. Melt grape jelly and chili sauce together in microwave (using equal amounts of jelly and chili sauce). Pour over frozen meatballs in a 9 x 13 pan. Cover with foil. Bake in oven for 30 minutes. Serve in chafing dish with toothpicks! ∿

—*Nadine originally got this recipe years ago from Operations Technician Gary Carlson. Nadine's a working Mom so easy recipes are a must! It's now part of the annual New Year's Eve celebration. Make it a tradition in your family as well.*

Nadine and Bruce Felt are the proud parents of two beautiful children, Connor and Nicole. It's the role of mother that Nadine cherishes more than anything. While family is the number one priority, Nadine makes time for many local charities (this is just one of many!). She previously sat on the board of the Crisis Pregnancy Center and was instrumental in the effort to create a maternity home in Spokane for unwed mothers. Nadine also received the 2000 Family Honors Award in Media from the Northwest Families Council for involvement in organizations that strengthen families. Nadine is one of those people that makes the community a better place. While she originally hails from Vancouver, WA, she's now a full-fledged Spokanite. We plan on keeping Nadine for years to come!

You may know Nadine Woodward as an important part of the KREM 2 anchor team (catch her at 5:00, 6:00, 10:00, and 11:00) but she's part of an even more important crew, her family.

Hot Mushroom Dip

INGREDIENTS:

3	Tbsp. butter
1	lb. mushrooms, sliced
1	large onion, chopped
1½	cup mayonnaise
10	strips bacon, fried and crumbled
¼	tsp. seasoned salt
½	cup cheddar cheese

1 Preheat oven to 350°.

2 In a skillet, sauté mushrooms in butter for 3-5 minutes. Combine all ingredients except cheese in ovenproof dish. Cover with cheese.

3 Bake 25 minutes. Serve with toasted bread points. ✎

—*Bev Bemis sends us this recipe from her Coeur d'Alene, ID, kitchen.*

Crab Dip

INGREDIENTS:

1	8 oz. pkg. cream cheese, softened
½	cup mayonnaise
½	cup onion, chopped
½	cup celery, chopped
2	Tbsp. lemon juice
2	Tbsp. creamed horseradish
1	Tbsp. Worcestershire sauce
1	8 oz. can cooked crabmeat, chopped

1 Blend cream cheese and mayonnaise in bowl. Add remaining ingredients except crabmeat. Mix well.

2 Stir in crab. Chill covered for 2 hours or longer. Serve with chips or crackers. ✎

—*This recipe is from Dorothy Campbell.*

Crab Dip

Janet Baret of Spokane Valley makes her crab dip with a little twist. She combines 1 8 oz. pkg of cream cheese with a jar of Kraft Pimento Cheese. She stirs in 2 Tbsp. mayonnaise, 2 Tbsp. lemon juice, and 4 dashes of Worcestershire sauce (add garlic salt if desired). Once well blended (add a tiny bit of milk if needed to blend) she adds 1 small can of crabmeat. Refrigerate for several hours and serve with crackers or veggies. ✎

Quick Fix

Pickled Eggs

INGREDIENT:	
2	cups vinegar
1	cup sugar
1½	tsp. dry mustard
2½	tsp. course salt
1	Tbsp. pickling spice
10	hard boiled eggs, shelled

In a saucepan, bring vinegar, sugar, mustard, salt, and pickling spice to a boil. Remove from heat. Pour liquid over shelled eggs in a bowl or large jar. Let marinate for a few days and eat! ∾

—Fern McLennan watches KREM 2 from her home in Redcliff, Alberta. That's also where she whips up this recipe for pickled eggs.

Deviled Eggs

INGREDIENTS:	
10	hard boiled eggs
¾	cup mashed potatoes (prepared with skim milk and margarine)
1	Tbsp. fat free mayonnaise
1	tsp. prepared mustard
2-3	drops yellow food coloring
	Paprika

1 First; slice eggs in half lengthwise and remove yolks. Use 2-3 yolks for this mixture and refrigerate the rest for a different use. Set aside whites.

2 In a small bowl; combine mashed potatoes, egg yolks, mayonnaise, mustard, and food coloring if desired. Mix well. Stuff or pipe into egg whites. Sprinkle with paprika. Refrigerate and serve. ∾

—This recipe from Mrs. William Pace of Clarkston, WA, uses mashed potatoes. It takes deviled eggs to a whole new level!

Quick Fix

Cocktail Sauce

If you have some shrimp, here's a cocktail sauce to serve it with. It's sent in by Margie Shepherd of Spokane. She combines 1 cup catsup, 1 Tbsp. lemon juice, 1 Tbsp. Worcestershire sauce, and 1 Tbsp. horseradish. Mix and refrigerate. ∾

Cheese Spread

Jacqueline Karnes of California was visiting her daughter here in Spokane and wanted to send in this cheese spread recipe. It's simple. Combine 8 oz. cream cheese (room temperature) with 8 oz. spreadable cheddar cheese. Add 2 Tbsp. mayonnaise. Salt and pepper to taste. Combine ingredients with a mixer. Refrigerate and serve with crackers. ❧

Avocado Dip

INGREDIENTS:	
6	oz. cream cheese, softened
2	ripe avocados
1	tsp. garlic powder
1	Tbsp. lemon juice
2	Tbsp. mayonnaise

Combine cream cheese, avocados, garlic powder, and lemon juice. Blend well. Add mayonnaise. Chill for at least one hour. Serve with chips. ❧

—Evelyn Larkin from Spokane sent in this recipe. It's quick and easy!

Salmon Pate

INGREDIENTS:	
1	7¼ oz. can salmon
1	envelope Italian dressing mix
1	8 oz. pkg. cream cheese

1 Line a 2-cup bowl or small loaf pan with plastic wrap. In a separate bowl, combine ingredients. Press mixture into container lined with plastic wrap.

2 Cover and chill at least 1 hour. Unmold and serve with crackers or cucumber slices. ❧

—Corinne Hirst of Spokane sent us this recipe for a salmon pate that would be a perfect beginning to a lovely dinner.

Crabby Sandwich Appetizers

INGREDIENTS:	
8	oz. imitation crab meat
⅓	cup mayonnaise
¼	cup sour cream
¼	cup green onion, chopped
¼	cup celery, finely chopped
1	Tbsp. lemon juice*
1	hard-boiled egg, chopped
½	tsp. dill weed
¼	tsp. black pepper

In a bowl, combine all ingredients. Serve on toast points, biscuit halves, or puffed pastry. ∾

* If doubling recipe do not double lemon juice.

—Thanks to Karen Tice of Bonners Ferry, ID, for sending us this appetizer. Add a salad and this could almost make a meal!

In news... always lead with the best.

Crab Stuffed Mushrooms

INGREDIENTS:	
24	medium mushrooms
2	Tbsp. green onion, minced
5	Tbsp. butter
1	tsp. lemon juice
1	cup cooked crabmeat, flaked
½	cup soft bread crumbs
1	egg, slightly beaten
½	tsp. dill weed
¾ to 1	cup jack cheese, grated

1 Preheat oven to 400°.

2 Wipe and clean mushrooms. Remove stems and finely chop. In a skillet, sauté chopped stems with onions and butter. Remove from heat. Stir in lemon juice, crab, breadcrumbs, egg, dillweed, and ¼ cup of cheese.

3 Melt remaining butter in a 9 x 13 pan. Turn mushroom caps in the butter to coat. Spoon about 1 Tbsp. of mixture into each mushroom cap.

4 Place filled mushrooms filled-side up in baking dish. Sprinkle with remaining cheese. Bake for 15-20 minutes. ∾

—Irene Van Leuven sent us this recipe from her kitchen in Colbert, WA. They can be prepared the day before a big party and cooked at the last minute.

Crab Meat Puffs

INGREDIENTS:

Fillings:

1	**7 oz. can crab meat, drained and flaked**
1	**celery stalk, finely chopped**
½	**small onion, minced**
¼ to ½	**cup mayonnaise**
	Salt and pepper
	Lemon juice
	Worcestershire sauce

Puffs:

½	**cup butter**
¼	**tsp. salt**
1	**cup boiling water**
1	**cup sifted flour**
3	**eggs, unbeaten**

1 Preheat oven to 400°.

2 To make puffs; add butter and salt to boiling water. Bring mixture back to boil over medium heat.

3 Lower heat; add flour all at once and beat vigorously until mixture leaves sides of the pan. Add one egg at a time, beating thoroughly after each addition. Remove from heat.

4 Place balls of mixture (approx. 1 tsp. each puff) on cookie sheet. Bake for 10 minutes at 400°. Reduce heat to 350° and let bake about 30 minutes longer. Remove from oven and cool.

5 To make filling, combine all ingredients together.

6 To assemble puffs; make a slit on side of each puff and fill with crab mixture. Serve! ∾

—Dee Taylor sent us in this recipe. It takes a few minutes to make but well worth the effort.

Clam Dip

INGREDIENTS:

1	**8 oz. pkg. cream cheese, softened**
½	**cup Miracle Whip**
1	**Tbsp. Catalina French dressing**
⅓	**cup onion, finely chopped**
1	**small can minced clams, drained and dry**

Mix all ingredients together and serve with chips or crackers. ∾

—Mary Kay Lutes of Bonners Ferry, ID, sent in this easy recipe for clam dip.

Sesame Chicken Wings

INGREDIENTS:	
3	cups soy sauce
1	tsp. ground ginger
1	cup packed brown sugar
2	cups Sauternes (sweet white wine)
3	garlic cloves, crushed
4	dozen chicken wing drumettes
1	cup sesame seeds

1 Preheat oven to 400°.

2 In a saucepan, combine soy sauce, ginger, brown sugar, wine, and garlic. Bring to a boil. Reduce the heat and simmer for 30 minutes. Add the chicken drumettes and simmer for 15 minutes while stirring occasionally.

3 Remove drumettes with slotted spoon. Sprinkle with sesame seeds. Place wings on baking sheets and cook for 15 minutes. They should be served hot and crispy. (If you want to make wings in advance; follow directions up to the point where you coat in sesame seeds. Cover with foil and refrigerate until 30 minutes before your ready to cook in the oven.) ∾

—Arlene Mortensen of Spokane says her wings are tried and true. Make them tonight and find out why they are a favorite!

Chili Con Queso

INGREDIENTS:	
1	lb. ground beef
1	8 oz. can tomato sauce
2	Tbsp. green onion
1	4 oz. can chili peppers
1	tsp. Worcestershire sauce
2	lbs. jack cheese
1	large bag tortilla chips

1 In a skillet, brown ground beef over medium heat. Add tomato sauce, green onion, chili peppers, and Worcestershire sauce. Simmer for about 10 minutes.

2 Pour mix into preheated crock-pot. Cut cheese into one inch chunks and add to crockpot. Let mix cook on high for about an hour. Serve warm with tortilla chips. ∾

—This recipe was submitted by Mike & Dawn Veilleux. Talk about comfort food on a cold evening.

Flour Tortilla Roll-ups

	INGREDIENTS:
2	8 oz. pkgs. cream cheese
1	pkg. ranch mix (dry)
2	green onions, tops chopped fine
1	jar diced pimento
1	can diced green chili peppers
1	small can chopped black olives
8	flour tortillas

In a bowl, mix all ingredients except for tortillas. Spread mixture on tortillas. Roll. Wrap in plastic and refrigerate for at least two hours. Slice crossways into 1-inch pieces. Serve. ∾

—Jean Kimm of Coeur d'Alene, ID, sent us this recipe for an easy no-bake appetizer. It makes a lot and your guests will gobble them up.

Cornucopia Roll-ups

	INGREDIENTS:
1	3 oz. pkg. cream cheese
1	Tbsp. curry powder
½	cup pecans, finely chopped
2-3	Tbsp. milk
	Pepper
12	slices turkey or ham (luncheon meat)

In a bowl, combine cream cheese, curry, and pecans. Stir in milk until moistened. Season with pepper to taste. Spread mixture onto lunch meat slices and roll. Refrigerate and serve. ∾

—This recipe was sent in by I.M. Glendenning of Spokane.

Stuffed Mushrooms

Bev Saul sent us this easy recipe for stuffed mushrooms. She removes and chops the stems of 1 pound of cleaned mushrooms. She combines the stems with ½ cup parmesan cheese (grated), ¼ cup melted butter, and 2 Tbsp. of chopped green onion. She divides ingredients among the mushrooms. Bev slips them under the broiler until caps are crusty. Serve hot! ∾

Quick Fix

Bar-B-Q Water Chestnuts

INGREDIENTS:

1	8 oz. can whole water chestnuts, drained
½	lb. bacon
	Toothpicks
½	cup catsup
⅓	cup brown sugar

1 Preheat oven to 325°.

2 Cut bacon slices in half. Wrap each water chestnut with a piece of bacon and secure with toothpick. Place on baking sheet.

3 In a small bowl, combine catsup and brown sugar. Pour mixture over water chestnuts. Bake for 30-35 minutes. ∾

—Delores Jones of Spokane Valley sent us this recipe. It only uses a few ingredients and is a warm way to start your dinner.

Quintin's Party Mix

INGREDIENTS:

5	cups popped popcorn
8	cups corn chips
4	cups cheese crackers
3	cups mixed nuts
1½	cups walnuts or pecans
½	lb. butter (no substitutes)
½	tsp. garlic powder
½	tsp. curry powder
1	Tbsp. Worcestershire sauce
	Several dashes of Tabasco

1 Preheat oven to 250°.

2 In a large bowl; combine popcorn, corn chips, crackers, and nuts. In a saucepan, melt butter. Add garlic powder, curry powder, Worcestershire sauce, and Tabasco. Pour butter over popcorn mixture. Toss well.

3 Spread onto baking sheets. Bake for 1 hour. Stir occasionally. Drain on paper towels when done baking. Cool and store in airtight containers or freeze. ∾

—Marjorie Landreth sent us this recipe from her Spokane kitchen. The recipe makes a lot and can be stored in the freezer.

Roasted Garlic

Take a head of garlic and peel off outer layer of skin. Cut off the top of the cloves of garlic. Place bulb in a baking dish and lightly coat garlic with olive oil. You can throw in some fresh rosemary if desired. Cover the dish tightly with foil and bake for about 45 minutes at 350°. Uncover and bake a few more minutes or until garlic is desired consistency. Cool until you can handle the cloves with your hands. Peel off the individual cloves and squeeze out garlic onto bread or crackers. ❧

Cheese Bread Spread

INGREDIENTS:

1	lb. margarine, whipped
½	lb. sharp cheddar, grated
¼	lb. romano cheese, grated
1	tsp. Worcestersire sauce
¼	tsp. garlic powder
½	tsp. paprika
1	loaf French bread (sliced lengthwise or slices)

1 Mix margarine, cheddar, romano, Worcestersire, and garlic powder well. Spread over bread. Sprinkle with paprika.

2 Broil until the cheese is hot and bubbly. Serve immediately. ❧

—OK, you're definitely not going to lose weight on this recipe but you'll have a good time starting a party with this cheese bread. It was sent in by Kathy & Roger Premo and Bill & Donna Cole.

Zucchini Pancakes

INGREDIENTS:

1½	cups shredded zucchini
1	egg, lightly beaten
2	Tbsp. baking mix
3	Tbsp. parmesan cheese, grated
	Pinch of pepper
1	Tbsp. cooking oil

1 In a bowl, combine zucchini, egg, biscuit mix, cheese, and pepper. Over medium heat, warm oil in a skillet.

2 Drop batter onto skillet (a ¼ cup at a time). Fry until golden brown. Turn and cook other side. ❧

—I.M. Glendenning sent us this recipe. We thought it would make a nice appetizer or first course. Though a few of these with a tossed salad could make a whole meal.

Chili, Soups and Stews

Grandpa Jobie's Chili

	INGREDIENTS:
5	lbs. chuck roast
¾	lb. beef fat
1	med. onion (chopped)
2	tsp. crushed garlic
1	Tbs. ground cumin
2	small cans tomato sauce
3	oz. paprika
4	oz. chili powder

For best results cook in oven, however this can be done in a crock-pot as well.

1 Cut meat into chunks. Brown in a large pot. Chop fat fine.

2 Put fat, onion, garlic, cumin and tomato sauce in oven pan (or crock-pot) with lid. Add water to cover meat ⅔ up the pan.

3 Cook for 4 hours in oven at 250°, or crock-pot on high. Add chili powder and paprika and cook for another hour.

4 Add more chili powder and paprika to taste.

—This recipe was submitted by KREM 2 Operations Manager Dan Lamphere. It's a chili recipe that tastes fantastic when cooked in the oven.

▲ The KREM 2 Operations Department is made up of more than two dozen talented employees. These people handle the day-to-day technical jobs needed to keep KREM 2 on the air. From the KREM 2 studio, control room, and master control, operations employees oversee local and national broadcasts every minute of the day to ensure viewers receive the best-looking programs possible on both our analog and digital program streams. Several employees have served KREM 2 for more than three decades working first in film, then videotape, and finally, digital servers. Whether part-time or full-time, seasoned or new, every operations employee is an important member of a large team that helps make KREM 2 a great place to work.

From left to right: **Bob Phillips** has been at KREM 2 for more than 30 years. He currently runs audio for our primetime newscasts. You may also recognize him as the voice of KREM. **Katie Parish** is a director and graphic artist. **Dan Lamphere** is our Operations Manager. We call him our technical guru. **Naci Seyhanli**, one of our many Eastern Washington University alumni, directs our primetime newscasts.

Ralph's Chili and Beans

INGREDIENTS:	
1	lb. dry beans (red or black)
4+	cups water
2	Tbsp. dry beef broth
1	Tbsp. dry vegetable broth
⅓	cup dry wheat berries
3½	lbs. ground pork
3	Tbsp. chili powder
2	Tbsp. paprika
4	whole chives, chopped
2	Anaheim peppers, chopped
½	red bell pepper, chopped
2	large garlic cloves, finely chopped
½	tsp. cumin seeds
1½	tsp. oregano
¾	lbs. salsa
	Grated cheese (optional)

KREM 2's Laura Papetti loves to cook! Really, she loves to eat. Her real coup-de-gras is her dad's chili recipe. She even brought home the blue ribbon at the Montana State Fair with the recipe. Growing up in the Papetti household was a culinary treat. Her mother, Leslie, is a gourmet cook who entertains constantly, and her dad, Ralph, designs his own chili, soup, and cereal recipes. Even her brother Randy is a fantastic cook, and his wife Gina lets him have full range in the kitchen. Laura was raised in Anchorage, Alaska. That's where she met her husband Greg Heister who benefits from Laura's cooking obsession. They both like living in the Northwest where they enjoy adventuring in the outdoors with their favorite pal Roosevelt (a very naughty Boston Terrier).

1 Soak beans overnight in water. Do NOT throw away water after soaking. Cook beans in the two kinds of broth with just enough of the soaking water to cover beans. Cook for about 45 minutes, adding wheat berries the last 20 minutes.

2 In a different, large stockpot, cook pork until all pink color is gone. Remove all the fat. The best method is to use a turkey baster. Save this fat/juice mix in a bowl. After fat mixture cools, the white fat will solidify on top. Discard fat and add the broth to the bean mixture.

3 To the pork; add the chili powder, paprika, chives, Anaheim peppers, red bell pepper, garlic, cumin, and oregano. Sauté until peppers begin to soften. Add salsa. Pour bean mixture into pork mixture. Simmer at a low temperature for about 45 minutes. Add more water if necessary. Stir every 5 minutes to avoid scorching. Add salt and/or your favorite hot spice to suit your taste. Remove from heat. Top with grated cheese! ❧

—This recipe was submitted by Laura Papetti.

Tomato Vegetable Soup

INGREDIENTS:	
1	small onion, chopped
1	stalk celery, chopped (about ½ cup)
1	Tbsp. (heaping) butter
1	box dry instant tomato with basil soup (Knox brand recommended)
2	Tbsp. dry vegetable flakes
3	mushrooms, chopped
2	green onions, sliced with tops on
4	cups water
2	roma tomatoes, chopped
3	tomatillas, chopped
2	whole allspice
3	whole peppercorns
	Fresh ground pepper
	Sour cream

Put all the ingredients except sour cream in a large kettle and cook until celery and onion are soft. It takes about 20 minutes. Serve up in large bowls with a dollop of sour cream. ◠

—Marylin Tibbett sends us this soup recipe from her Spokane kitchen. The dry soup mix gives instant flavor!

Vegetable Beef Soup

INGREDIENTS:	
1	lb. ground beef
1	cup onion, diced
1	cup raw potato, cubed
1	cup carrots, sliced
½	cup celery, diced
1	cup cabbage, shredded
2	cups tomatoes (1 lb. can)
1½	qt. water
1	small bay leaf
½	tsp. thyme
¼	tsp. sweet basil leaves
4	tsp. salt
¼	tsp. pepper
¼	cup rice or 1/2 cup elbow macaroni

In a large kettle, brown ground beef with onion. Add potatoes, carrots, celery, cabbage, tomatoes, water, and spices. Bring to a boil; add rice or macaroni. Cover and simmer for 1 hour. ◠

—Vonda Aamodt of Kellogg, ID, sent us this recipe for a vegetable beef soup. With warm bread it's a perfect meal on a winter afternoon.

Quick Fix

Bo Soup

James Bohannon of Deer Park, WA, sent us this easy soup recipe with just a few ingredients. In a large stockpot, he combines 6 large onions (chopped), 2 green peppers (diced), 2 large tomatoes (fresh or canned, diced), 1 large head of cabbage (chopped), 1 large bunch of celery (sliced), and 1 pkg. of dry onion soup mix. He covers the mixture with water and brings it to a boil for about 30 minutes. Soup's on! ◠

Cheddar Chicken Chowder

INGREDIENTS:	
4	bacon slices
1	lb. boneless chicken breast
1	cup onion, chopped
1	cup red pepper, diced
1	cup celery, diced (optional)
2	garlic cloves
2	cups peeled red potatoes, diced
4½	cups chicken broth
2½	cups frozen corn
⅓	cup flour
2	cups milk (or half and half)
¾	cheddar cheese, shredded
½	tsp. salt
¼	tsp. pepper

1 In a stock pot, cook bacon and crumble. Set bacon aside. In bacon drippings; combine chicken, onion, red pepper, celery, and garlic. Sauté for 5 minutes. Add broth and potatoes and cook for 20 minutes. Add corn and stir well.

2 In a separate bowl, combine flour and milk. Add mixture to soup. Simmer 15 minutes while stirring frequently. Stir in cheese, salt, and pepper. Top with bacon. ∾

—This recipe was sent in by Tex Gaston of Spokane. He says it's easy and delicious!

Taco Soup

INGREDIENTS:	
1½	lb. hamburger, browned and drained
1	small onion, chopped
1	pkg. taco seasoning
1	28 oz. can kidney beans, drained and rinsed
1	16 oz. can corn, with juice
1	16 oz. can tomato sauce
1	16 oz. can diced cooked tomatoes
2-3	tsp. chili powder (optional)
½	tsp. garlic powder (optional)
	Taco chips
	Cheese, grated
	Sour cream

In a stockpot, combine the onion and seasoning with the browned meat. Add the beans, corn, tomato sauce, and diced tomatoes. Add spices if desired. Simmer for about an hour. ∾

—We received several recipes for taco soup. Sharon Dale of Elk, WA, along with Helen Prenguber and H. Irene Matson (both of Spokane) all sent in similar recipes. Helen says you can adjust the ingredients to what you have on hand. Irene uses a dash of chili powder and garlic powder to liven up her recipe, while Sharon serves her soup with chips, cheese, and sour cream. We combined them all into this recipe that is sure to please.

Scrumptious Lentil Soup

	INGREDIENTS:
½	cup onion, chopped
1	garlic clove, chopped
½	lb. lentils (or 1½ cups)
6	cups water
2-3	carrots, chopped
2	medium potatoes, chopped
1	cup tomato juice
½	tsp. parsley
1	tsp. salt
	Pepper
½	tsp. oregano
½	tsp. thyme

1 In a skillet, sauté onion and garlic in butter or olive oil until onion is transparent.

2 Meanwhile, in a stockpot cook lentils in water for 30 minutes or until lentils are tender. Add sautéed onions and garlic to stockpot. Add carrots, potatoes, tomato juice, parsley, salt, pepper to taste, oregano, and thyme.

3 Bring to a boil. Reduce heat and simmer until vegetables are tender. ∾

—Paula Rose of Mica, WA, sent us this recipe for lentil soup. She adapted it from a recipe out of a cookbook. We're glad she included her version in our cookbook!

Cool Cucumber Soup

	INGREDIENTS:
1	medium cucumber, peeled and diced
1	onion, thinly sliced
½	cup water or ice cubes
¼ to ½	cup lowfat yogurt
	Salt
	Lemon juice
	Dill weed (optional)

In a blender, combine cucumber, onion and ice cubes and blend until a slushy consistency. Add to taste salt, lemon juice, and dill weed (if desired). Fold in yogurt until desired consistency. Serve chilled. ∾

—Lois Moore of Spokane sent us this soup recipe that's perfect on a hot day! Soup is not just for winter.

A hot story always makes the news

Old Fashioned Beef Stew

INGREDIENTS:	
1	lb. lean beef chuck, trimmed and cut into 1-inch cubes
2	Tbsp. flour
2	tsp. vegetable oil
2	large yellow onions, thinly sliced
2	garlic cloves, minced
2	tsp. reduced sodium tomato paste
¾	cup beef broth
4	cups carrots, sliced
2	medium russet potatoes, thinly sliced
1	cup green bean pieces, 1-inch slices (can use celery if desired)
1	Tbsp. cornstarch
1	Tbsp. cold water
¼	cup fresh parsley (optional)

1 Coat beef with flour, shaking off excess. In a large nonstick pot, heat oil over medium-high heat. Add beef; sauté until browned, about 6 minutes. Place on plate.

2 Add onions and garlic to pot; sauté, stirring for 1 minute. Pour off fat. Return beef to pot; stir in tomato paste, then broth.

3 Add enough water to just cover; bring to a boil. Reduce heat to low; simmer until beef is tender, about 1 and 15 minutes.

4 Skim off any foam. Add carrots, potatoes, and green beans. Cover partially; simmer for 15-30 minutes.

5 In a small bowl, mix cornstarch and cold water; stir into stew. Increase heat and boil uncovered for 1 minute. Sprinkle with parsley (if desired) and serve. ∽

—This hearty stew recipe comes from Diana Hancock Ridley.

Barley Beef Stew

INGREDIENTS:	
1	lb. ground beef
1	onion, diced
1	cup celery, diced
1	cup carrots, sliced
1	cup potatoes, diced
½	cup barley
4-5	beef bouillon cubes
2	tsp. salt
4	cups water

In a large stockpot, brown ground beef. Push to one side and add onion and celery. Sauté until soft. Stir in remaining ingredients and bring to a boil. Cover, reduce heat and simmer for 1 hour or until barley is tender. ∽

—Cheryl Van Den Hazel of Nine Mile Falls, WA, sent in this stew recipe that adds barley.

San Antonio Stew

INGREDIENTS:	
2	lbs. stew meat, cubed
2	Tbsp. vegetable oil
1	cup beef broth
1	cup hot water
1	8 oz. jar picante sauce
1	small onion, chopped
1	tsp. salt
1	tsp. cumin
2	garlic cloves, minced
1	16 oz. can tomatoes
3	carrots, chopped
1	10 oz. package frozen corn
1	lb. zucchini, sliced
½	cup cold water
2	Tbsp. flour

1 In a Dutch oven, brown meat. Add broth, hot water, picante sauce, onion, salt, cumin, and garlic. Simmer for 1 hour.

2 Add tomatoes, carrots, corn, and zucchini. Cook about 25 minutes. In a small bowl, combine cold water and flour. Add to stew. Stir until thickened. ∾

—Spokane's Jack Powers sent in this recipe that gets some kick from picante sauce.

Hunter's Stew

INGREDIENTS:	
¼	cup flour
1	tsp. paprika or caraway seed
1	lb. lean beef, cubed
1	lb. lean pork, cubed
2	Tbsp. butter or margarine
2	lbs. sauerkraut, rinsed and drained
2	medium onions, sliced
1	12 oz. polish sausage, 1-inch cubes
1	4 oz. can mushrooms, undrained
½	cup white wine
	Vegetables of choice (optional)
	Small boiled potatoes (optional)
	Parsley, chopped (optional)

1 Combine flour and paprika. Coat meat pieces. Heat butter in a Dutch oven or stockpot. Add meat and brown on all sides. Add sauerkraut, onion, sausage, mushrooms, and wine.

2 Mix together and cook over low heat 1½ to 2 hours. Meat should be tender. Remove meat to a serving platter. If desired, serve with vegetables, potatoes and parsley. ∾

—This recipe was sent in by Wes Reed of Colfax, WA. You won't go away hungry.

Linda's Chili

INGREDIENTS:

2	lbs. lean hamburger
1	lb. hot Italian sausage
1	large onion, chopped
4	garlic cloves, chopped
1	bottle of beer
2	cups beef or chicken stock
2	32 oz. cans chopped tomatoes, undrained
2	8 oz. cans tomato sauce
2	8 oz. cans kidney beans
½	cup mild chili powder
1	Tbsp. cumin
1	tsp. salt
1	tsp. pepper

1 In a large stockpot; brown hamburger and drain off fat. In same pot; brown sausage and reserve a small amount of drippings. Sauté onions and garlic in sausage drippings until soft.

2 Add the beer and stock, stir to loosen drippings in pan and bring to a boil. Lower heat and simmer 10-15 minutes. Add remaining ingredients and simmer on very low temperature or crockpot for 3-4 hours. ✎

—Linda Oswald says she makes this chili recipe for large family gatherings or hunting trips in the Fall. You may want to invite your friends and family over today!

Fred's Best Ever Bean Medley

INGREDIENTS:

1	lb. bacon
2	large onions, chopped
½	cup vinegar
½	cup brown sugar
1	tsp. garlic salt
1	tsp. dry mustard
1	can kidney beans, drained
1	can lima beans, drained
1	can butter beans, drained
2	cans pork and beans

1 Preheat oven to 350°.

2 In a stockpot, fry bacon until crisp. Remove from pan, crumble bacon and return pieces to pan. Add onions and sauté until translucent. Add vinegar, brown sugar, garlic salt, and mustard. Simmer for 20 minutes.

3 Mix beans and sauce into oven-proof pot or baking dish. Cook uncovered for 1 hour. ✎

—This recipe was submitted by Claudia Stoffel. She says it goes fast when served hot or cold.

Neoma's Party Beans

	INGREDIENTS:
1	3 lb. 5 oz. can pork and beans
1	large Walla Walla Sweet Onion, chopped
1	green pepper, chopped
1	15 oz. can kidney beans
1	15 oz. can butter beans (can substitute with lima beans)
1	32 oz. can stewed tomatoes
1	cup catsup
1	cup packed brown sugar
½	cup prepared mustard

Strain beans from their juices. Add ½ all beans to crock-pot. Add all other ingredients and then layer with the rest of the beans. Stir gently. Cook on low for 4 hours. ✎

—Neoma Mauget sent us this recipe. She says you can add some green chilis if you want to give it kick. She cooks hers in a full-sized crockpot.

Ranch Style Baked Beans

	INGREDIENTS:
2	Tbsp. butter
1	lb. ground chuck
2-3	onion slices, chopped
1	envelope dry onion soup mix
½	cup water
2	lb. cans pork and beans in tomato sauce
1	1 lb. can kidney beans, drain
1	cup catsup
2	Tbsp. prepared mustard
2	tsp. cider vinegar

1 Preheat oven to 400°.

2 In a large skillet, melt butter. Brown ground chuck and onions. Add dry soup mix and water.

3 Add, pork and beans in tomato sauce, kidney beans, catsup, mustard, and cider vinegar. Mix until well blended.

4 Pour mixture into 2½ qt. casserole dish. Bake for 30-45 minutes. ✎

—Lois Hogan makes this baked bean recipe in her Spokane kitchen.

Dennis' Favorite Baked Beans

INGREDIENTS:	
2	1½ lb. cans of pork and beans
1	cup brown sugar
2	tsp. dry mustard
4	slices bacon, cooked and crumbled
1	cup catsup

1 Preheat oven to 350°.

2 Mix all ingredients together and place in a casserole dish. Bake for 1 hour at 350°.

3 Turn heat down to 300° and continue to cook for another 1-2 hours or until thickened. ∾

—Sandi Miller of Pasco, WA, sent us this recipe for baked beans.

Pineapple Barbecue Beans

INGREDIENTS:	
1	lb. ground beef, browned and drained
1	medium onion, chopped
1	green pepper, chopped
1	garlic clove, minced
1	tsp. soy sauce
1	28 oz. can baked beans
1	cup barbecue sauce
1	small can pineapple chunks, with juice
	Salt and pepper

1 Preheat oven to 350°.

2 Mix all ingredients together. Place in a baking dish. Bake for 45 minutes. ∾

—Mary and Gay Wandler sent in this recipe for a different kind of bean concoction.

Lena's Baked Beans

Everyone has a favorite bean or chili recipe. Lena Hill combines: 1 can pork and beans, 1 can kidney beans, 1 can baby lima beans, 1 can barbecued beans, 1 lb. pork sausage, browned and drained, 1 can crushed pineapple, 1 medium chopped onion, 1 diced apple, ½ cup hot chili sauce or catsup, and ½ cup molasses. She bakes the mixture for 2 hours at 350°. Serve cold or hot. ∾

Quick Fix

Chili de Casa (Chili of the House)

INGREDIENTS:

1½	lb. chicken breast, diced
1	medium onion, diced
1	jalapeno pepper, seeded and diced
3	Tbsp. cooking oil
2	Tbsp. chili powder
1	Tbsp. instant coffee
4	Tbsp. flour
1	cup water
1	15 oz. can diced tomatoes
1	8 oz. can tomato sauce
1	cup salsa (medium heat)
1	15 oz. can black beans, drained
1	15 oz. can pinto beans, drained
½	sweet red pepper, diced
	Pepper sauce, to taste

1 In a large pot, brown chicken, onions, and jalapeno pepper in oil. Add chili powder, coffee, flour, and water. Stir to mix. Cook on low heat for 1 hour.

2 Add diced tomatoes, tomato sauce, and salsa. Heat thoroughly. Add black beans, pinto beans, and red pepper. Add pepper sauce if needed. ✎

—Robert Nelson of Hayden Lake, ID, says this chili recipe is 40 years in the making. It has evolved into a family favorite. Make it for your family.

Hawaiian Bean Pot

INGREDIENTS:

1	lb. 13 oz. pork and beans
1	8 oz. can pineapple tidbits, drained
1	Tbsp. soy sauce
2	Tbsp. instant toasted onion
½	tsp. Old Hickory smoked salt
1	4.5 oz. jar whole mushrooms, drained
⅓	cup brown sugar
1	Tbsp. orange zest or grated peel
2	Tbsp. catsup

1 Preheat oven to 350°.

2 In a large bowl; mix all ingredients together. Pour into 1½ qt. casserole dish. Bake for 1 hour. ✎

—Helen Ray says this recipe is always requested by friends. Helen is from Veradale, WA.

Mexican Seafood Soup

INGREDIENTS:	
1	3 lb. can chopped clams
1½	cups water
3	cubes chicken bouillon
⅔	cup wild rice
½	cup millet
1-2	Tbsp. olive oil
1	onion, chopped
2	Anaheim peppers, cut into small pieces
1	bell pepper (orange, yellow, or red) cut into small pieces
1	cup chopped chives
6	garlic cloves, finely chopped
2	Tbsp. dried oregano
1½	tsp. rosemary, ground by hand
4	lbs. salsa, chunky
1½	cups artichoke hearts (oil soaked), cut into pieces
15	green olives, quartered
1½	lb. cocktail shrimp, fresh or frozen
	Hot sauce to taste
	Salt to taste

Brett Allbery loves two things. His family and good food. When Brett isn't working as a photojournalist he is spending time with his beautiful little girl (Samantha—a favorite around KREM 2) and his wife Kristine. Brett and his wife graduated from Gonzaga University and have always called Spokane home. Brett also plays soccer and each year sweats it out on the Hoopfest court. Brett stole this recipe from co-worker Laura Papetti. She stole it from her Dad. As they say, all is fair in love and food.

1 Drain water from can of clams into large pot. Do not put clams in yet. Add 1½ cups water, bouillon cubes, wild rice and millet. Cover pot. Simmer rice mixture on low heat until cooked (cooking time for wild rice will vary—read rice packet instructions).

2 In a different large pot, heat olive oil. Slightly sauté onions, Anaheim peppers, bell pepper, and chives. Add garlic, oregano, and rosemary. Sauté very briefly. Add salsa and clams. Cook for about 10 minutes.

3 To salsa mixture; add cooked wild rice and millet mixture. Cook another 10 minutes.

4 Add artichoke hearts, olives, and shrimp. Cook on low temperature for about 15 minutes. As soon as onions and peppers are cooked remove from heat as to not overcook shrimp.

5 Spice it up with a little salt and hot sauce if desired. Enjoy. ∾

—Recipe submitted by Brett Allbery

Salads and Sides Dishes

Spinach Almond Salad

INGREDIENTS:	

Salad:

6	Tbsp. sugar
1	cup almonds
1	lb. fresh spinach
1	cup strawberries, sliced
1	cup green grapes, halved
1	11 oz. can mandarin oranges, drained

Dressing:

⅓	cup cider vinegar
⅓	cup vegetable oil
¼	cup sugar
1	Tbsp. dijon mustard
1	tsp. salt
½	tsp. pepper
½	small onion, chopped
2	tsp. poppy seeds

Don't take this the wrong way. We love Melissa Phillips as a reporter. She's great! But when it comes right down to it we really like her cooking. She's a journalist by trade but a chef at heart.

Melissa learned to cook from her Grandma Lorna. Melissa originally hails from Salt Lake City, Utah, but has lived all over the United States (before Spokane she was in Alaska!). She completed her undergraduate degree at the University of Utah and received her masters from University of Missouri. When not at work or in the kitchen, Melissa loves to spend time with her cat, Mitchell. She also loves to bike, golf, ski, and knit.

1 For salad: Pour sugar and almonds into heavy saucepan. Heat until sugar melts and coats almonds. Pour onto wax paper and break apart with fork while still hot. Set aside and cool.

2 Wash spinach and pat dry. Tear into bite sized pieces and place in bowl.

3 For dressing: combine all the ingredients and mix well.

4 To serve: Just before serving combine salad ingredients and top lightly with dressing. ∿

—*Melissa Phillips*

24-Hour Cabbage Salad

	INGREDIENTS:
1	large cabbage, cut fine
3	medium onions, sliced
1	cup sugar
¾	cup cooking oil
1	cup vinegar
1	tsp. salt
1	tsp. dry mustard
1	tsp. celery seed
2	Tbsp. sugar

1 In a large bowl; put a layer of cabbage and a layer of onions until all ingredients are used. Pour sugar over layers. DO NOT STIR.

2 Meanwhile, in a saucepan combine oil, vinegar, salt, dry mustard, celery seed, and sugar. Bring to a boil. Pour over cabbage and refrigerate for 24 hours without stirring. Mix and eat. ∿

—*Agnes Moberg from Hayden Lake, ID, sent us this easy salad recipe.*

French Dressing

Judy Budleski from Hauser Lake, ID, sent us this recipe to dress up your everyday salad. She combines 2 cups olive oil, 2 cups catsup, ½ cup vinegar, 4 tsp. lemon juice, 1¼ cup sugar, 2 tsp. salt, 2 tsp. paprika, and 1 tsp. dry mustard. Blend ingredients well and store in a covered mason jar in the refrigerator. ∿

Quick Fix

Pea and Peanut Salad

INGREDIENTS:	
2	small pkgs. frozen peas
1	small can spanish peanuts
1	tsp. lemon juice
2	cups sour cream
1	tsp. Worcestershire sauce
	Dash garlic salt

1 Lay out peas on a paper towel to thaw. Pat dry. In a bowl, mix peas and peanuts together.

2 Add lemon juice, sour cream, Worcestershire sauce, and garlic salt. Let stand for 2-3 hours before serving. ∾

—This recipe was sent in by Barbara Miller of Spokane. She says she got the recipe from her girlfriend after moving here from Michigan.

Crunch Salad

INGREDIENTS:	
1	head cauliflower
1	bunch broccoli
4-6	green onions
1	can water chestnuts
1	10 oz. pkg. frozen peas (rinsed)
1	pkg. Good Seasons cheese-garlic dry mix
1	cup sour cream
1	cup mayonnaise

1 Cut or break cauliflower, green onions, and water chestnuts into bite-sized pieces. Add rinsed green peas.

2 Make a dressing of cheese-garlic mix, sour cream, and mayonnaise. Mix with vegetables. ∾

—This recipe is from Barbara Pedersen of Othello, WA.

Quick Fix

Carrot Salad

Charlotte Perin likes to make this salad as a healthy snack for her kids. She mixes 4 cups of grated carrots with a 14 oz. can crushed pineapple (drained), 1 cup raisins, and a container of pineapple or vanilla yogurt. Refrigerate and serve! ∾

Poppy Seed Salad Dressing

Terri Snyder of Chewelah tosses her salad with this easy dressing. She combines ⅓ cup strained honey, ½ tsp. salt, ⅓ cup vinegar, 3 tsp. mustard, 1¼ cup vegetable oil, and 2½ Tbsp. poppy seeds. Mix ingredients in the order given. Beat in an electric blender until oil seems to disappear. ❧

Crunch Corn Medley

INGREDIENTS:

2	cups frozen peas
1	can whole kernel corn, drained
1	can white corn, drained
1	8 oz. can water chestnuts, drained and chopped
1	4 oz. jar diced pimentos, drained
8	green onions, thinly chopped
2	celery ribs, chopped
1	medium green pepper, chopped
½	cup vinegar
½	cup sugar
1	tsp. salt
¼	tsp. pepper

1 In large bowl, combine peas, corn, chestnuts, pimentos, green onions, celery, and green pepper. In a small bowl, combine vinegar, sugar, salt, and pepper.

2 Pour liquid mixture over vegetables. Cover and refrigerate for at least 3 hours before serving. ❧

—This summer salad is perfect for potlucks according to Mary Romjue of Spokane.

Carrot Salad or Relish

INGREDIENTS:

2	lbs. carrots, peeled and sliced
1	can tomato soup
½	cup sugar
½	cup oil
½	cup vinegar
1	tsp. salt
1	tsp. pepper
1	onion, chopped
1	green pepper, chopped

1 Cook carrots until tender, but crisp. In a saucepan, bring soup, sugar, oil, vinegar, salt, and pepper to a boil.

2 Pour over carrots. Add onion and green pepper. Chill overnight in refrigerator. ❧

—This dish sent in by Jean Martin of Chattaroy, WA, can be served as a salad or side dish.

Chinese Chicken Salad

INGREDIENTS:		
Dressing:		
2	Tbsp.	corn starch
4	Tbsp.	water
½	cup	vinegar
½	cup	water
½	cup	catsup
12	Tbsp.	sugar
1	Tbsp.	soy sauce
Salad:		
4		chicken breasts, cooked, cut into small chunks
½		pkg. wonton skins
1		lettuce head, sliced
½		bunch green onions, sliced
1		pkg. slivered almonds

1 Dressing: To make the sauce combine cornstarch and water together. Then add all ingredients to a saucepan. Heat through for about 15 minutes until sauce becomes transparent. Remove from heat and cool. Carefully pour into jar and refrigerate.

2 Salad: Place chicken chunks in large bowl. Meanwhile, slice wonton wraps in ⅛" strips and fry until crispy. Add to chicken. Add lettuce and green onions to bowl. Cover with dressing and mix thoroughly. Serve. ❧

—*Charlotte Senn of Spokane says she learned this recipe back in Home Economics class in the 1970's. Years later, it's still a hit!*

Sesame Salad

INGREDIENTS:		
Dressing:		
3	Tbsp.	rice vinegar
1	Tbsp.	sesame seed oil
½	tsp.	pepper
2	Tbsp.	sugar
1	tsp.	salt
2	Tbsp.	vegetable oil
Salad:		
1		head Romaine lettuce
4		green onions, chopped
½		cup radishes or carrots, sliced
1		large chicken breast, cooked and diced
3		Tbsp. toasted sesame seeds
½		cup rice noodles

1 Dressing: Combine all ingredients together in a large measuring cup or small bowl.

2 Salad: Combine all salad ingredients together in a large bowl. Cover with dressing. Serve. ❧

—*This recipe sent in by Velma Dehnel of Moses Lake, WA, uses sesame seeds and rice noodles.*

Hot Crab Lentil Salad

INGREDIENTS:

	Saltines, crushed to cover bottom of 9x9 pan
	Butter
1	green pepper, diced
1	small onion, diced
1	can shrimp
1	can crab
4	hard-boiled eggs, diced
1	cup mayonnaise
1	tsp. Worcestershire sauce
½	cup cooked red lentils (cooked until soft)

1 Preheat oven to 350°.

2 Line bottom of 9 x 9 baking dish with buttered, crushed Saltine crackers. Cover the whole bottom of dish. In a mixing bowl, combine all the other ingredients.

3 Pour mixture over crushed saltines. Cover mixture with more crushed saltines. Bake for 45 minutes. ❧

— A perfect salad for a cold day. This was sent in by Stacie Burns of Colfax, WA.

Ted's Papaya Salad

INGREDIENTS:

1	cup salad oil
⅓	cup tarragon vinegar
¼	cup sugar
½	tsp. salt
½	tsp. dry mustard
½	tsp. instant minced onion
1	cucumber, peeled and sliced
2	Tbsp. papaya seeds
1	papaya peeled and sliced
3-5	cups mixed greens
2	Tbsp. lime juice (or the juice of 1 fresh lime)

1 Place salad oil, sugar, lime juice, salt, dry mustard, minced onion in a blender. Blend thoroughly. Add papaya seeds and blend until seeds resemble coarse pepper. Add cucumber slices and papaya to mixed greens. Toss with dressing. ❧

—Submitted on behalf of Ted McGregor Sr. Ted is known in the McGregor clan for his exceptional salads. He recommends soaking the mixed greens in an ice water bath to crisp the lettuce, and then uses a salad spinner to dry the greens.

Pineapple Pecan Chicken Salad

INGREDIENTS:

1	lb. chicken (or turkey), cooked and cut into bite size pieces
1	8 oz. can chunk pineapple, drained (reserve juice)
¾	cup green or red seedless grapes
½	cup pecan halves
½	cup raisins
1	red apple, cut into small cubes
1	Tbsp. lemon juice
1	pkg. Top Ramen noodles
½	cup Miracle Whip
½	cup celery

1 In a large bowl, combine chicken, pineapple, grapes, pecans, and raisins. Sprinkle apples with lemon juice. Add apples to mixture.

2 Break noodles (uncooked) into mixture. Add seasoning from noodle package. Add Miracle Whip, pineapple juice, and celery. Toss thoroughly to mix. ❧

—*The recipe was sent in by Lorene Hemperly of Spokane.*

Five Bean Salad

INGREDIENTS:

Dressing:

¾	cup sugar
½	cup salad oil
1	tsp. salt

Salad:

1	can yellow beans
1	can green beans
1	can red kidney beans
1	can soy beans
1	can garbanzo beans
1	small onion, chopped
1	green pepper, chopped
1	red pepper, chopped
1	small head cauliflower, diced

1 Dressing: In a jar combine the dressing ingredients.

2 Salad: Combine all the beans and vegetables in a bowl. Cover with dressing mixture. Refrigerate overnight. Serve. ❧

—*Vivian Taylor of Hayden, ID, sent in this recipe for a five bean salad. If you're short a bean or two… that's O.K! She says it will still be tasty.*

Apple Grape Salad

INGREDIENTS:

2	large apples, chopped (peel is optional)
½	tsp. salt
1	cup seedless grapes, cut in half
½	cup chopped dates
¼	cup pecans, chopped
6	oz. french vanilla yogurt

Dip apples in salt, drain well to keep fruit from turning brown. Mix the rest of the ingredients in with apples. ✻

—Arlene Clauson of Priest River, ID, sent us this recipe that uses yogurt as the dressing.

Broccoli Salad

INGREDIENTS:

4	stalks broccoli, cut into bite sized pieces
10	slices bacon, cooked and crumbled
5	green onions, thinly sliced
1/4	cup raisins
1	cup mayonnaise
2	Tbsp. red wine vinegar
1/4	cup sugar

In a large bowl, combine broccoli, bacon, green onions, and raisins. In a small bowl, mix mayonnaise, red wine vinegar, and sugar together. Pour dressing over vegetables and chill for at least 1 hour before eating. ✻

—Davenport's Kitty Bullinger sent us this recipe.

Greek Tomato Salad

INGREDIENTS:

2-3	large tomatoes, cubed
1	can Greek or black olives, chopped
8	oz. feta cheese, cut into small chunks
1	large garlic clove, chopped
2	Tbsp. lemon juice and pulp
2	Tbsp. olive oil
2	Tbsp. oregano, chopped
	Salt
	Black pepper

1 In a large bowl, place tomatoes, olives, feta, and most of the garlic.

2 In a small bowl, combine remaining garlic, lemon juice, olive oil, oregano, salt, and pepper. Let lemon juice mixture set for at least 15 minutes. You can add more garlic depending on preference.

3 Mix juice mixture in with tomato mixture. Stir several times. Place in refrigerator for at least 1 hour. ✻

—This recipe comes from the kitchen of Frank Yuse.

Kansas Cucumber Salad

INGREDIENTS:	
1	cup mayonnaise
¼	cup sugar
4	tsp. white vinegar
½	tsp. dill
½	tsp. salt
4	cucumbers, peeled and sliced thin

Toss all ingredients together. Cover and chill for at least 1 hour. ❧

—Katherine Higgins from Colfax, WA, sent in this easy recipe that uses only a few ingredients.

Salada de Palmito

INGREDIENTS:	
1	16 oz. can hearts of palm, drained, cut into chunks
1/2	head romaine lettuce
	Croutons
	Salt, to taste
	Pepper, to taste
	Lemon juice, to taste
	Olive oil, to taste
1/4	cup parmesan cheese, shredded

Mix all ingredients in a large bowl and serve! ❧

—This is a delicious and easy recipe sent in by Susan Baker. She's Katie Fixter's Mom!

Baked Potato Salad

INGREDIENTS:	
4½	lbs. red potatoes, peeled and cut into chunks
¼	cup olive oil
2	envelopes dry Italian salad dressing mix
1	medium green pepper, chopped
1	bunch green onions, chopped
2	large tomatoes, chopped
4	hard-boiled eggs, chopped
5	bacon strips, cooked and crumbled
1½	cups mayonnaise
1	Tbsp. vinegar
1	Tbsp. lemon juice
2	tsp. dried basil
1	tsp. salt
½	tsp. pepper
¼	tsp. garlic powder

1 Preheat oven to 400°.

2 In a large bowl, toss the potatoes with the oil and dressing mixes. Place in two greased 9 x 13 baking dishes. Bake uncovered for 45 minutes (or until tender). Cool. Transfer potatoes to a large bowl; add peppers, onions, tomatoes, eggs, and bacon. Toss gently. In a small bowl, combine mayonnaise, vinegar, lemon juice, basil, salt, pepper, and garlic powder. Mix well. Pour over the salad and stir gently. Cover and refrigerate for at least 1 hour. ❧

—Tammy Fountaine of Veradale, WA, sent us this recipe that would be perfect for a picnic! It makes a lot for a whole crowd of hungry people.

Holiday Stuffing

INGREDIENTS:	
1	large loaf of white bread, toasted and cubed
2	cans chicken broth
1	can cream of mushroom soup
1	can cream of chicken soup
1	cup celery, chopped
1	cup onion, chopped
3-4	Tbsp. sage (or to taste)
	Salt, to taste
	Pepper, to taste

1 Preheat oven to 350°.

2 Pour chicken broth over toasted bread and stir. Let stand for about 15 minutes. Add soups, celery, onion, and seasoning.

2 Put stuffing in a 9 x 13 pan and bake covered for 30 minutes. Uncover stuffing and bake for another 30 minutes. ∽

—This recipe was sent in by Spokane's Dorothea Bennett. It's been in her family for more than 60 years.

Apple-Cheese

INGREDIENTS:	
1	stick butter (room temperature)
¾	cup sugar
8	oz. Velveeta Cheese
¾	cup flour
4-5	medium ripe apples; peeled, cored, and sliced
	Lemon juice
	Non-stick vegetable spray

1 Preheat oven to 350°.

2 Cream butter and sugar together gradually. Tear cheese into small pieces and add to creamed mixture. Blend well. Add flour gradually and blend. Spray a 9 x 9 baking dish lightly with non-stick spray. Place apples in bottom of pan. Pour a little lemon juice over apples to keep them from turning brown. Spread cheese mixture over apples by hand (do a little finger painting!) with some swirls on top. Be careful to keep apples 'tucked in' under the mixture. It's pretty sticky so put it in your hands first and pull it out like pizza dough, loosely covering the apples. Spread to the edge by hand. Bake for 30-40 minutes until the top is brown. ∽

—This recipe comes from the family of KREM 2's very own Barbara Grant. She runs our business office but also enjoys her role as mother of 12-year-old Shelby.

Dresden Mushrooms

INGREDIENTS:	
1	lb. pork sausage
2	pkgs. mushroom gravy mix
1	cup water
2	lbs. button mushrooms
2	large onions, sliced
1	can mushroom soup
1	cup sherry

1 In a large-deep skillet, brown pork sausage. In a small bowl, combine gravy mix and water. Add mixture to sausage. To sausage mixture, add mushrooms, onions, soup, and sherry.

2 Cook slowly until mushrooms are soft and chewy. It takes about 4 hours. Serve over rice, with biscuits, or as a side dish. ∾

—Marilyn Walters of Spokane sent in this recipe for what she calls 'Dresden Mushrooms'. To understand the name you have to know the story.

"We were lost in Dresden, Germany, when we stumbled upon an outdoor bazaar," writes Marilyn. "These mushrooms were served from a sidewalk booth. I have tried to duplicate the recipe." If it is not accurate, it is a very nice substitute-in our opinion.

Sausage Dressing

INGREDIENTS:	
1	lb. sausage
3	qts. bread cubes, toasted
1¼	tsp. salt
1	cup celery, chopped
¼	cup onion, chopped
2	Tbsp. poultry seasoning (or sage)
1½	cup boiling water (up to 2 cups)

In a skillet, brown sausage until partly crisp and crumbled. Pour sausage and drippings over dry ingredients. Mix well, but gently. Add hot water until desired consistency. Enough to stuff a 10-16 lb. bird. ∾

—This recipe was sent in by Spokane's Dorothy Larsen.

It's the special dressing that makes the story good.

Barbecued Green Beans

INGREDIENTS:

4	cans french cut green beans, drained
4	strips bacon, crumbled plus drippings
1	cup catsup
1	cup brown sugar
1	medium onion, sliced

1 Preheat oven to 225°.

2 In a skillet, brown bacon and onion. Place beans in a baking dish. Add bacon and drippings. Mix in catsup, brown sugar, and onion. Bake covered for 4 hours. You can also cook in a crock-pot on slow all day. ∾

—*This recipe was sent to us by Geraldine Miller, from Nezperce, ID.*

Marinated Onions

INGREDIENTS:

½	cup water
½	cup vinegar
1½	cups sugar
5-6	onions, sliced
2	tsp. celery seed
1	cup mayonnaise

In a saucepan, bring water, vinegar, and sugar to a boil. Meanwhile, place onions in a baking dish. Pour liquid mixture over onions and let sit overnight. In a small bowl, combine celery seed and mayonnaise. Mix this into onions. Serve. ∾

—*Naida Pritchard sent us one of her favorite recipes! She makes it while cooking in her Greenacres, WA, kitchen.*

Cranberry Jello Salad

Bena Mathews of Colville, WA, sent us this easy recipe. She combines 1 6 oz. pkg. cranberry jello, 2 cups boiling water, 1 cup 7-Up, 1 can whole berry cranberry sauce, and 2 cans mandarin oranges. Pour into mold and let set in refrigerator. ∾

Quick Fix

My Mom's Rice Pilaf

INGREDIENTS:	
¾	cube butter (no substitutes)
6	green onions, chopped
½	lb. fresh mushrooms, sliced
1	cup white rice (not instant)*
2	cans beef stock (consommé)
1	soup can water

1 Preheat oven to 375°.

2 Sauté onions and mushrooms in butter. Add rice, soup, and water. Stir a little. Put mixture into a 9 x 13 baking dish. Making sure the rice is evenly distributed bake for 45 minutes or until rice is done. You may want to stir once or twice while baking. ❧

*Brown rice will take longer. Add 1/2 soup can water extra.

—Vikki Thatcher sent in this recipe and it's no guess who she stole it from!

Marge's Easy Potatoes

INGREDIENTS:	
2	lbs. hash browns, thawed
1	8 oz. carton sour cream
2	cans cream of potato soup
1	8 oz. Old English Cheese, grated
½	cup Parmesan cheese, separated into 1/4 cups

1 Preheat oven to 300°.

2 Mix all ingredients together, reserving ¼ cup of parmesan cheese. Put in a greased 9 x 13 baking dish. Top with reserved cheese. Bake for 1½ hours at 300°. Turn to 350° if needed to brown top. ❧

—Marge Batson sent us this recipe. She says it can be put together and refrigerated overnight if you want to have less preparation when entertaining.

Quick Fix

Sweet and Sour Salad Dressing

This recipe was sent to us by Edwin LaMotte of Malott, WA. He combines ½ cup red wine vinegar, ½ cup water, 2 oz. red garlic vinegar, and 3 pkgs. of Equal. Salt and pepper to taste. ❧

Rice Side Dish

Doreen Hess sent us this side dish from her Hayden, ID, kitchen. This is a handy recipe if you have leftover rice. Take 1 cup of cold cooked rice and mix with ⅓ cup sugar, 1 cup drained crushed pineapple, ½ tsp. vanilla, ⅓ cup miniature marshmallows, and 2 tablespoons of chopped maraschino cherries (drained). Fold in 1 cup of whipping cream. Chill for a couple of hours before serving! ❧

Company Carrots

INGREDIENTS:

5	cups carrots, sliced
1	cup sour cream
1	3 oz. pkg. cream cheese
3	Tbsp. green pepper
2	Tbsp. green onions
½	tsp. salt
½	tsp. lemon peel, grated
⅛	tsp. pepper

1 Cook carrots until tender in salted water. Drain.

2 Combine with remaining ingredients. Heat thoroughly and serve. ❧

—This recipe was sent in by Edith Foedish of Spokane.

Zucchini Patties

INGREDIENTS:

3	cups zucchini, grated
2	eggs, well beaten
1	cup Bisquick
1	cup grated cheese
½	tsp. salt

In a bowl, combine all ingredients together. Take mixture and form into patties the size of small pancakes. Fry in oil until crisp on each side. Serve warm or cold. ❧

—This recipe was sent in by Ruby Poage of Spokane.

Main Dishes

Barbecued Pork Spareribs

	INGREDIENTS:
2	lbs. pork spareribs (boneless if desired)
1	cup onions (chopped)
1	Tbsp. butter
½	cup water
2	Tbsp. vinegar
1	Tbsp. Worcestershire sauce
¼	cup lemon juice
2	Tbsp. brown sugar
1	bottle Heinz Chili Sauce
½	tsp. salt
¼	tsp. paprika

1 Preheat oven to 450°.

2 Cut spareribs into serving size pieces. Place in a baking pan and cook for 15 minutes at 450°. Remove ribs and pour off fat. Reduce oven to 350°.

3 While ribs are baking; sauté onions in butter. Add water, vinegar, Worcestershire sauce, lemon juice, brown sugar, chili sauce, salt and paprika. Simmer for 15 minutes.

4 Pour ingredients over the meat and bake the ribs for 1 hour at 350°. Baste frequently. Serve and watch your family smile! ∾

— Recipe submitted by Randy Shaw. He stole it from his mother, Phyllis Burrows.

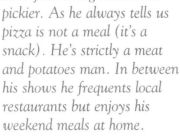

Randy Shaw, Spokane and news are all synonymous. The award-winning journalist has covered everything from the Watergate hearings to a National Geographic expedition to Africa. When it comes to food though he's much pickier. As he always tells us pizza is not a meal (it's a snack). He's strictly a meat and potatoes man. In between his shows he frequents local restaurants but enjoys his weekend meals at home.

Even at age six Randy dreamed of being a singing cowboy just like his heroes: Roy Rogers and Bud Burrows. This picture was taken at the family's Spokane ranch.

Mandarin Chicken

INGREDIENTS:	
2-3	lbs. chicken breasts
¼	cup flour
2	Tbsp. margarine
2	Tbsp. oil
4	Tbsp. lemon juice
½	cup orange juice
2	Tbsp. honey
½	Tbsp. soy sauce
½	tsp. powdered ginger
1	11 oz. can mandarin oranges, keep juice
	Cornstarch

1 Wash and dry chicken. Put flour in a paper bag and coat chicken — one piece at a time. In skillet, heat margarine and oil; add chicken and brown each piece.

2 Drain mandarin oranges and reserve liquid in a small bowl. Mix mandarin juice with lemon juice, orange juice, honey, soy sauce and ginger. Pour over chicken in skillet. Cover and simmer for 35 minutes or until chicken is tender.

3 Add mandarin sections 5-6 minutes before the chicken is cooked through. After removing chicken pieces, you can slightly thicken sauce with cornstarch and serve over hot rice. ❧

— This recipe is from Phyllis Burrows. She's Randy Shaw's Mom and she knows how to cook! No wonder Randy is always so happy.

Aunt Terry's Chicken Casserole

INGREDIENTS:	
6	cooked chicken breasts
1	can cream of mushroom soup
1	can cream of chicken soup
1	cup milk
1	dozen corn tortillas
½	bottle green taco sauce (any size)
3	cups grated sharp cheddar cheese
1	medium chopped onion

1 *The Night Before:* Mix soups, taco sauce and milk. Shred the cooked chicken. Pour some of the soup mixture into a 2 qt. casserole dish (just enough to cover the bottom of dish). Using 1-3 tortillas, tear them up into big pieces and place on top of the sauce. Add a layer of shredded chicken and cover with a layer of cheese. Top with a thin layer of sauce. Lay down more torn tortillas, chicken and repeat the layers. The last layer should be cheese. Cover and refrigerate overnight.

2 *Next Day:* Bake covered at 350° for 45 minutes. Uncover and bake for another 15 minutes or until it is warm in the center. ❧

— This recipe was sent in by Christine Boone from Albion, Washington. Her Aunt Terry came up with the recipe many years ago and the family has enjoyed it ever since. You actually build the casserole the night before so it's perfect for entertaining.

Chicken Cacciatore

INGREDIENTS:	
1	cut up fryer chicken (3-4 pounds)
1	Tbsp. olive oil
6	oz. mushrooms, finely chopped
1	medium onion, finely chopped
1-2	cloves garlic
¾	cup dry white wine
2	Tbsp. white wine vinegar
¾	cup chicken broth
1	tsp. salt
¼	tsp. pepper
1	qt. stewed tomatoes
1	15 oz. can tomato sauce
8	Italian Greek olives
1½	tsp. dried basil
¾	tsp. dried marjoram
1	Tbsp. chopped parsley
	Angel hair pasta

1 Rinse chicken, drain and pat dry with paper towels. Heat oil in a large skillet. Add chicken and cook over medium heat for 8 minutes per side or until browned. Remove chicken to dutch oven. Leave your drippings in the skillet. Press the tomatoes through a sieve, discard seeds, set juice aside.

2 Add mushrooms and onions to drippings in skillet. Cook and stir over medium heat for about 5 minutes or until onion is softening. Add garlic, stir and cook for 30 seconds. Add wine and vinegar and cook over medium heat for about 5 minutes or until liquid is almost evaporated. Stir in broth, salt, pepper, basil and marjoram. Add tomato juice from stewed tomatoes and tomato sauce mixture. Bring to a boil over medium-high heat. Reduce to low, cover and simmer for 30 minutes.

3 Bring sauce back to a boil, cook over medium high heat for 5 minutes. Add olives and parsley to sauce and cook 1 more minute. Serve sauce over chicken and pasta. ∾

— Bill Cusick sent this recipe in from Spokane. He says this family favorite makes lots of sauce so you can save some and freeze it for a quick meal in the future. Sounds good to us!

Quick Fix

Poppyseed Chicken

Having lots of guests but little time to cook? Try this recipe sent in by Helen Crain of Coeur d'Alene, ID.

- Chop up 6 cooked chicken breasts and put them into a 9 x 13 pan.

- Mix 8 oz. of sour cream and 1 can of cream of chicken soup. Spread over the chopped chicken. Mix 1¼ cup crushed Ritz Crackers and 1 Tbsp. of poppyseeds. Sprinkle on top of chicken mixture. Drizzle ½ cup melted butter on top. Cook for 40 minutes (or until bubbly) at 350°. ∾

Chicken with Warm Bean Salsa

	INGREDIENTS:
4	skinless chicken breasts
½	tsp. dried oregano
¼	tsp. salt
⅛	tsp. freshly ground pepper
¾	cup shredded cheddar cheese
1	14½ oz. can mexican-style stewed tomatoes
1	15 oz. can of black beans, rinsed & drained
2	Tbsp. chopped cilantro

1 Spray large non-stick skillet with cooking spray. Sauté chicken until lightly browned (about 3 minutes). Sprinkle with oregano, salt and pepper. Turn over and sauté until chicken is cooked through.

2 Sprinkle with 1 Tbsp. of cheese. Meanwhile, in a small saucepan, bring tomatoes and beans to a boil.

3 Serve chicken, topped with black bean salsa and remaining cheese and cilantro. ∾

— Joan Ryan of Spokane sent in this delicious (and easy!) recipe. Though it doesn't have a lot of ingredients, it's filled with flavor.

Spanish Style Chicken

	INGREDIENTS:
1	Tbsp. olive oil
1	lb. skinless, boneless chicken thighs
½	tsp. salt
½	tsp. pepper
1	16 oz. package frozen stir-fry vegetables
1	14½ oz. can diced tomatoes, undrained
1	cup uncooked long-grain rice
1	cup water
½	cup dry sherry
½	tsp. rosemary
2	Tbsp. drained capers
2	Tbsp. minced fresh parsley

1 Heat oil in a dutch oven over medium-high heat. Sprinkle chicken with salt and pepper then add to pan. Cook 6 minutes browning all sides.

2 Stir in vegetables, tomatoes, rice, water, sherry and rosemary. Bring to a boil then reduce heat and simmer for 22 minutes or until liquid is nearly absorbed.

3 Stir in capers and parsley. Cover and let stand for 5 minutes. (4 servings). ∾

(Exchanges: 2½ starch, 1½ vegetable, 2 lean meat)

— Jill Strickland sent in this healthy chicken recipe. She says it's a dish for diabetics but anyone will love it!

Chicken Bake

This easy recipe was sent in by FeLecia Boudy.

§ FeLecia prepares 1 can of cream of chicken soup. She also boils 4 boneless, skinless chicken breasts for 1 hour. She places chicken into a baking dish and adds half of the soup mixture, 1 lb. of cooked broccoli and 4-6 cups of cooked rice. She heats dish in the oven for about 20 minutes on 350°. Salt and pepper to taste. ∾

Chicken Rice Bake

INGREDIENTS:	
2	cups raw rice
1	chicken
2	cans of cream of mushroom soup
2	cans of milk
1	pkg. of dried onion soup
2	small cans of mushroom pieces

1 Preheat Oven 350°.

2 Spread 2 cups of raw rice into an 8 x 12 baking dish. Add 1 cut up chicken.

3 In bowl, mix 2 cans of cream of mushroom soup, 2 cans of milk, 2 cans of water, and 1 pkg. of dried onion soup. Add 2 small cans of mushroom pieces. Pour over chicken. Cover with foil and bake for 1½ hours. ∾

— *This simple recipe was sent in by Jo Orahood of Spokane.*

Salsa Chicken with Spanish Rice

INGREDIENTS:	
1	lb. cooked chicken cut into chunks
1½	cup Minute Rice
¾ to 1	cup salsa
1	14 oz. can chopped tomato
½	cup apricot-pineapple jam
1	pkg. taco seasoning
1¾	cup hot water

1 Mix rice and 1½ cup of the hot water and ½ pkg. taco seasoning in medium saucepan.

2 When cooked, stir in 1 cup of the tomatoes and half the salsa. Heat through and turn off burner. Cover with lid.

3 In another pan combine chicken with ¼ cup water, jam, remaining taco seasoning and remaining tomatoes. Heat and serve with rice. ∾

— *Linda Mullen from Omak, WA, sent in this recipe that uses Apricot-Pineapple jam to spice up her chicken.*

Dutch Oven Almond Chicken

INGREDIENTS:

½	lb. fresh mushrooms
1	Tbsp. butter
1	whole chicken
¾	tsp. red cayenne pepper
½	Tbsp. garlic pepper
½	Tbsp. lemon pepper
1½	cups Italian breadcrumbs
½	cup chopped almonds
½	Tbsp. basil
½	tsp. ground oregano
3	eggs
¼	cup buttermilk
¼	tsp. salt
¼	lb. grated Monterey Jack cheese

1 Slice and sauté mushrooms in butter. Cut up chicken and remove skin. Wash, pat dry and coat all sides with the different peppers. Let chicken stand for 10 minutes.

2 Mix eggs, buttermilk and salt. Immerse chicken into mixture.

3 Mix breadcrumbs, about 3/4's of the almonds, basil and oregano in a separate dish. Roll chicken into the dry mixture and coat all sides. Place coated chicken into dutch oven or baking dish. Cover the chicken with mushrooms and remaining almonds.

4 Cover the dutch oven or baking dish and bake for 50 minutes at 350°. Uncover the chicken and bake for another 20 minutes. Sprinkle with cheese and let stand for 5 minutes and serve. ∾

(You can double or triple the recipe depending on how many people you are serving)

— Veradale resident Neva Talbot says she created this recipe from years of cooking in the backcountry with a dutch oven. Whether you're indoors or out, we think you'll love it.

Faux Fried Chicken

Judy Sauter of Coeur d'Alene sent in this recipe that is simple and delicious.

§ Judy recommends using any skinless chicken parts you want and dipping them in buttermilk. Then she rolls them in seasoned flour (flour with a little salt and pepper). She then dips it back into the buttermilk and rolls it in a mixture of corn flake crumbs and parmesan cheese. Arrange chicken on a baking pan sprayed with non-stick coating. Bake at 375° for 45-60 minutes (no pink in the middle). ∾

Quick Fix

Cranberry Chicken

INGREDIENTS:	
1	Tbsp. butter or margarine
1	small onion, chopped
3	lbs. chicken thighs (or parts of your choice)
⅔	cup catsup
⅓	cup packed brown sugar (light or dark)
1½	Tbsp. cider vinegar
1	tsp. dry mustard
2	cups fresh or frozen cranberries

1 Preheat oven to 400°.

2 Melt butter in skillet and sauté onions until golden (about 8-10 minutes).

3 Place chicken in baking pan. Pour butter and onion mixture over chicken and bake for 25 minutes.

4 In a separate bowl, stir together remaining ingredients. Spoon mixture over chicken and bake an additional 20 minutes until cranberry mixture is slightly carmalized and chicken is no longer pink in middle. ∾

(If you use other chicken parts besides thighs cooking time may vary.)

— Norma Graber of Colville, WA, sent this recipe in for cranberry chicken. It's a perfect Fall or Winter dish when the cranberries are piled at every store.

Honey Mustard Chicken

Joanie Carrier of Cheney, WA, sent in this easy and flavorful chicken recipe.

§ Joanie mixes ½ Cup of Dijon mustard, ⅓ cup honey, 2 Tbsp. fresh dill (or 1 Tbsp. dry dill) and 1 tsp. of orange peel. She coats 2½ pounds of chicken (parts of your choice) with the mixture, making sure to brush a little under the skin. Bake the chicken at 400° in a foil-lined baking dish for 30 minutes (or until juices run clear). ∾

Grandma's Feather Dumplings

This was sent in by Valjean Chambers of Spokane.

- Mix together 2 cups of flour, 1 tsp. salt, 4 tsp. baking powder, ¼ tsp. pepper, 1 beaten egg, 3 Tbsp. melted butter, and ⅔ cup milk. Form small balls out of the mixture. Drop into a simmering pot of chicken broth (2 cups broth). Cover with lid for 18 minutes. Don't remove lid until time is up! ↝

Quick Fix

Poor Man Salisbury Steaks

INGREDIENTS:

1	lb. ground meat (beef, chicken, turkey or pork)
½	cup crushed soda crackers (you can use oat meal or bread crumbs)
1	egg
⅛	tsp. salt
⅛	tsp. pepper
1	small onion, chopped
1	clove garlic, chopped
2	cans creams-style soup (set aside)
1	can water

1 Mix all ingredients in a large bowl except for the soup and water. Form patties and fry in small amount of oil on medium-high heat. Turn patties over when there is a crisp crust on one side.

2 In separate bowl mix the cream-style soup and the water until all lumps are gone. Pour mixture over patties and turn down heat to medium low. Simmer for 45 minutes. ↝

—Star Rowley sent this recipe in from Colville, WA.

Lazy Person's Roast

INGREDIENTS:

4	lb. rump roast
1	cup red wine
1½	tsp. salt
10	whole peppercorns
1½	Tbsp. brown sugar
2	bay leaves
½	tsp. dried sage

1 Preheat oven to 275°.

2 Trim fat from roast and place meat in a casserole dish. Add wine, salt, peppercorns, sugar and herbs. Cover tightly and cook for 4 hours at 275°.

3 Remove pan and let roast sit in its liquid for about an hour before serving. ↝

—James "Tracy" Stallard sent this recipe. We don't think he's lazy, just a time conserving cook!

Danish Meatballs

Marsha Sutton of Ephrata loves to make Danish meatballs and serve them over potatoes or rice.

§ Marsha mixes together ¾ lb. ground round, ¼ lb. mild sausage, 4 Tbsp. bread crumbs or oatmeal, 1 chopped onion , 1 egg (slightly beaten), and ¾ cup evaporated milk. Shape mixture into meatballs and bake on cooking sheet in the oven for 12 minutes at 350°. Meanwhile, mix together 1 can cream of mushroom soup with 1 can beef consommé and heat. Pour over meatballs and bake for another 30 to 40 minutes. Serve with rice or mashed potatoes. ❧

Ruth's Mexican Dish

INGREDIENTS:	
1	lb. ground beef
1	can chili (any kind)
1	can enchilada sauce (hot or mild)
1	pkg. shredded cheese
1	container sour cream
	Soft tortilla shells and chips

1 Preheat oven to 350°.

2 Brown the hamburger in skillet and drain oil. Add the enchilada sauce and olives. Line a 13 x 9 pan with crushed tortilla chips and pour the heated mixture over the chips and top with shredded cheese. Bake for 20 minutes or until cheese is bubbling. ❧

—Ruth Roberts says she's been enjoying this dish for years. We think you will too!

Homemade Sloppy Joes

INGREDIENTS:	
1	Tbsp. butter
1	lb. ground beef (or turkey)
½	cup chopped onion
1	medium green pepper, chopped
¾	cup catsup
¼	cup water
1	Tbsp. mustard
1	Tbsp. vinegar
	Salt and pepper
	Hamburger buns

In a skillet melt butter and brown meat. Add onion and green pepper. Add all remaining ingredients and simmer, uncovered, for 15 minutes. Serve on warm buns. ❧

—Laurie Meyer of Albion, WA, sent this recipe in for a homemade favorite. She says it's fast and easy.

Phineas Fogg's Worldly Stroganoff

	INGREDIENTS:
4	Tbsp. flour
½	tsp. salt
1	lb. top sirloin (cut into ½ inch strips)
4	Tbsp. butter, divided
1	cup sliced fresh mushrooms
½	cup chopped onion
1	clove minced garlic
3	Tbsp. tomato paste
1	can beef consommé
1	cup sour cream
2	Tbsp. sherry
1	lb. noodles (any shape)

1 Combine 1 Tbsp. flour and salt; roll meat strips in mixture. Melt 2 Tbsp. butter in a skillet and brown sirloin on all sides.

2 Add mushrooms, onion and garlic. Cook until onion is barely tender (about 5 minutes). Remove meat and mushrooms from pan. Melt other half of butter in pan drippings. Add 3 Tbsp. flour, stirring to avoid lumps. Add tomato paste. Pour in consommé and cook. Stir constantly until mixture thickens.

3 Return meat and mushrooms to skillet. Stir in sour cream and sherry. Heat mixture thoroughly but don't boil. Serve over noodles. ☙

—This recipe was sent in by Frances McCaffrey of Spokane.

Beef Curry

	INGREDIENTS:
¼	cup butter or margarine
4	large onions, chopped
4	garlic cloves, minced
¼	cup Indian curry powder
6	medium tomatoes, diced
3	Tbsp. tomato paste
2	cups water
2	lbs. lean beef, cubed (beef or lamb)
	Salt and pepper to taste
4	medium potatoes, diced
	Hot cooked rice (optional)

1 Melt butter or margarine in saucepan. Add onions and garlic. Sauté until golden, but not browned. Stir in curry powder and reduce heat. Cook over low heat 10 minutes to blend flavors. Add tomatoes. Sauté 3 minutes.

2 In a separate bowl, mix tomato paste with water. Pour tomato mixture into onions. Add meat, salt and pepper. Bring to a boil. Reduce heat and cover. Simmer over low heat for 1 hour.

3 Add potatoes. Cook covered 40 more minutes or until meat is tender. Serve over hot, cooked rice if desired. ☙

—Dale Fairweather from Trail, B.C., sends this recipe for curried beef. He says you can also use lamb. We like choices!

Carol's Sour Cream Enchiladas

INGREDIENTS:

Meat Mixture:

2½	lbs. ground beef, browned and drained
1	large onion, chopped
1	pkg. taco seasoning mix
1	can (1 lb. or 13 oz.) meatless chili

Sauce Mixture:
Mix following ingredients in a sauce pan:

1	can cream of chicken soup
1	pkg. Lipton onion soup
1	can cream of celery soup
1	4 oz. can chopped green jalapeno chiles
1	32 oz. sour cream

Toppings:

2½	cups grated cheese (cheddar or jack)
¾	cup green onion, chopped
1	can chopped olives

To Prepare Enchiladas:

1 Preheat oven to 325°.

2 Spray 2 large baking dishes with non-stick baking spray. Pour a little sauce into the bottom of dish and spread evenly.

3 Fill tortillas with a spoonful of meat mixture and roll up tortilla. Place in dish. Pour sauce mixture over enchiladas. Top with 2½ cups grated cheddar or jack cheese.

4 Bake for 30 minutes at 300- 325°. Garnish with chopped green onion and olives. ❧

—Carol Winter is from Coeur d'Alene, ID. This recipe made us hungry just typing it in.

Quick Fix

Baked Meatballs

Bena Mathews of Colville, WA, sent this recipe in for meatballs. This is comfort food at its best!

§ Make a box of Stove Top dressing (or any other brand) according to directions. Let dressing cool. Mix with 2 lbs. of ground beef. Add a little salt and pepper. Shape into meatballs and place on a 9 x 13 baking pan. Spoon 2 cans of cream of mushroom soup over the meatballs. Bake 1 hour at 350°. ❧

Kielbasa Casserole

Patricia Collier of Spokane likes to cut up one pound of Kielbasa into bite-sized chunks and combine it in a skillet with the following ingredients:

❧ Patricia combines ¾ cup uncooked converted rice, 1 can of condensed cream of celery soup, ¾ cup water, and 1 Tbsp. of butter. She covers the mixture and brings it to a boil. Reduce heat and simmer for 5 minutes. She then stirs in a 10 oz. pkg of frozen vegetables and a 2½ oz. can of sliced mushrooms (drained). She sprinkles the mixture with 1 cup of grated cheese and simmers for 20 minutes or until rice is cooked. ∾

Stuffed Green Peppers

INGREDIENTS:	
3	large green peppers
½	large onion, chopped
½	tsp. salt
1	lb. ground beef
½	cup instant rice
½	tsp. pepper
2	8 oz. cans tomato sauce
½	tsp. Tabasco
½	cup dry white wine
½	cup water
6	slices bacon, cut in half
¼	lb. sharp cheddar cheese, grated

1 Preheat oven to 350°.

2 Split washed green peppers in half lengthwise. Remove seeds and stems. Drop into lightly salted boiling water, turn off heat and let stand 5 minutes. Drain and arrange in baking dish.

3 Sauté onions in a small amount of butter or margarine until translucent. Mix onions, rice, ground beef, salt, pepper, and 1 can tomato sauce. Fill peppers with meat mixture.

4 Combine remaining can of tomato sauce with water, wine and Tabasco. Pour over peppers. Lay 2 slices of bacon halves on top of each meat filled pepper. Bake for 40 minutes. Sprinkle with grated cheese and return to oven for 20 minutes. ∾

—Donna Abbot's mom used to make this recipe when Donna was growing up. It's still a family favorite!

Quick Casserole

Need something quick! Vi Smith of Spokane recommends this casserole. Just four ingredients and minutes to make.

§ Vi browns 1 pound of ground round in a little cooking oil. She puts a layer of the meat inside a buttered casserole dish. Then she puts a layer of whole kernel corn (canned) on top of the meat. Vi adds a layer of tomatoes (canned) and a layer of cooked macaroni. She repeats the layering one more time. If you have a favorite cream sauce (or one in a can) you can put it on top and dot with a little margarine. Vi bakes the dish for 35-40 minutes at 350°. ∾

Pop Up Burger Pie

INGREDIENTS:	
Pie Filling:	
1½	lbs. lean ground beef
1	cup chopped onion
1	cup chopped green pepper
1	tsp. minced garlic
1	tsp. oregano
½	tsp. salt
1	tsp. pepper
1	15 oz. can tomato sauce
Batter:	
1	cup milk
1	Tbsp. olive oil
2	eggs
1	cup flour
½	tsp. salt
6	oz. mozzarella cheese, sliced
½	cup parmesan cheese, grated

1 Preheat oven to 400°.

2 In large skillet, brown the ground beef and drain well. Stir in onion, green pepper, garlic, oregano, salt, pepper, and tomato sauce; simmer 10 minutes, stirring occasionally. Set aside.

3 In small bowl, combine milk, oil and eggs. Beat 1 minute on medium speed. Add flour and salt; beat 2 minutes at medium speed or until well mixed. Pour hot meat mixture into 8" deep cast iron skillet. Top with sliced mozzarella.

4 Pour batter over mixture, covering the filling completely. Sprinkle with parmesan cheese. Bake for 25 minutes or until puffed and deep golden brown. Serve immediately. ∾

—Helen Meadows from Trout Creek, MT, sent this recipe in. She and her family raise cattle. We figured she knew a good beef recipe when she saw one.

Aunt Violet's Green Bean Casserole

INGREDIENTS:	
4	potatoes
1	lb. lean ground beef
1	medium onion, chopped
1	can tomato soup
½	can water
1	can drained green beans
	Seasoning salt

1 Preheat oven to 400°.

2 Peel, cut and boil potatoes until tender. While potatoes are boiling, brown hamburger in a large skillet with onion.

3 Once brown, sprinkle seasoning salt on meat. Add tomato soup, water, and green beans. Let simmer for a few minutes.

4 When potatoes are tender, mash them (make them on the dry side). Put meat mixture in 8 x 8 x 2 casserole dish.

5 Place 4 large spoonfuls of potatoes on top. Bake for about 20 minutes until potatoes are slightly brown on tips. ∾

—Bonnie Long of Post Falls, ID, says this dish has been a family favorite for 60 years. She says it's easy and economical. We like that it takes less than an hour to make!

Debbie's Lasagna

INGREDIENTS:	
3	lbs. ground beef
2	large onions, chopped
3	cloves of garlic, minced
1	28 oz. can tomatoes, crushed
1	Tbsp. Italian seasoning
½	cup parmesan cheese
1	16 oz. cottage cheese
1	box lasagna noodles
	Mozzarella cheese, grated

1 Preheat oven to 350°.

2 In skillet; brown hamburger, onion and garlic together. Drain fat. Add tomatoes, seasoning, parmesan, and cottage cheese and simmer for 15 minutes. Add salt and pepper to taste.

3 Meanwhile, cook noodles according to package (leave them a little firm). Put a layer of sauce in a 9 x 13 pan. Top with a layer of noodles.

4 Repeat steps until sauce and noodles are gone, ending with sauce. Top with mozzarella cheese and bake for 30 minutes. ∾

—Debbie Walter of Odessa, WA, sent in this recipe for lasagna. It's basic, easy and delicious. Try it on a cold night and you may wake up and have some for breakfast.

Green Beans Mexicali

INGREDIENTS:	
1	lb. lean ground beef
1	cup chopped red pepper
1½	cups French fried onions (divided)
⅓	cup salsa
1	cup grated cheese
1	14½ oz. can green beans (drained)
1	cup sour cream

1 Preheat oven to 350°.

2 Brown beef and red pepper together. Add salsa and grated cheese to beef mixture. Fold drained green beans into the mixture.

3 Meanwhile, slightly grease a 2 qt. casserole dish. Cover with half of the fried onions. Pour meat mixture over the fried onions. Cover and cook for 20 minutes or until heated through.

4 Remove. Spread sour cream on top of mixture and add the remainder of the fried onions. Do not cover. Cook for 5 more minutes. ∾

—*This recipe was sent in by KREM 2 viewer Hughena House of Spokane. She says it's a recipe that's won prizes. We say it's worth a ribbon!*

Mexican Lasagna

INGREDIENTS:	
1	lb. ground beef
¼	cup onion, chopped
1	14 oz. can tomato sauce
1	envelope taco seasoning
1	14 oz. can diced tomatoes, reserve liquid
1	pkg. 8-inch flour tortillas, cut into 2 inch strips
1	lb. cheddar cheese, shredded
1	can black olives, sliced (optional)

1 Preheat oven to 350°.

2 In skillet, brown hamburger and drain fat. Add onions, tomato sauce, diced tomatoes, and taco seasoning. Cook over medium heat for about 5 minutes.

3 In a 13 x 9 pan spread a layer of sauce. Cover with a layer of tortilla strip, sauce mixture, and cheese. Repeat layers finishing with sauce on top.

4 Sprinkle with remaining cheese. Bake for 40 minutes (or until bubbly). ∾

—*Lisa Tyler from Spokane is a busy mom of six! That said, she looks for easy recipes that can fill a family. She sent in this lasagna with a Mexican twist.*

A.J.'S Northern-Style Lasagna

INGREDIENTS:	
12-15	extra wide lasagna noodles
2½	lbs. extra lean ground beef
1	15-oz. can tomato sauce
1	lb. mozzarella cheese
1	lb. jack cheese
2	lbs. broccoli and cauliflower mix, medium cut pieces
	Salt, pepper and garlic powder
1½	Tbsp. Italian seasoning
1	Tbsp. taco seasoning
8	oz. water
2	Tbsp. cooking oil

1 Preheat oven to 350°.

2 Lightly brown ground beef. Do **not** season. Drain fat.

3 In a bowl, mix seasonings with tomato sauce and water. Pour seasoning mixture over meat and simmer until moisture is reduced. Stir frequently.

4 Meanwhile, cook vegetables in boiling water for 4-5 minutes. Set aside to cool.

5 Cook noodles until soft and tender. (A.J. recommends adding 2 Tbsp. cooking oil to noodles, while cooking.) In a baking dish (or lasagna pan), place half the meat sauce and cover with a layer of noodles. Add vegetables and cover with mozzarella cheese forming a cross.

6 Put jack cheese in the corners. Cover cheese with a layer of noodles. Layer with meat sauce and vegetables. On top, make a layer of cheese. Cover with foil; domed. Bake for 40-45 minutes. ∾

—We liked A.J. Denny's lasagna recipe because it was a bit different with a few vegetables thrown in.

Frito Tacos

INGREDIENTS:	
Brown together:	
2	lbs. ground beef
2	cloves minced garlic
1	large chopped onion
Drain grease from pan and add the following:	
1	cup cooked rice
2	cans tomato sauce
2	cans tomato paste
6	cans water (tomato paste cans)
¼	tsp. red pepper, pepper and salt
1	tsp. chili powder and oregano

Simmer for 2 hours. Serve over Fritos and top with chopped tomatoes, onions, lettuce and grated cheese. ∾

—Sally Pfeffer of Spokane sent this recipe in and says she doubles it and freezes it for later.

Baked Spaghetti

INGREDIENTS:

1½	lbs. hamburger
1	onion, chopped
1	cup green pepper, diced
1	28 oz. can diced tomatoes
1	4 oz. can mushrooms, drained
1	2¼ oz. can sliced olives
2	tsp. oregano
1	12 oz. package of spaghetti
1	can cream of mushroom soup
¼	cup water
2	cups cheddar cheese
¼	cup parmesan cheese

1 Preheat oven to 350°.

2 In a large skillet, brown the beef and drain. Add onion, pepper, tomatoes (with liquid in can), mushrooms, olives and oregano. Simmer together uncovered for 10 minutes.

3 Cook spaghetti according to package and drain all liquid. In a separate bowl combine soup and water until smooth.

4 Layer the bottom of a 9 x13 baking pan with half of the spaghetti. Spread half of the meat mixture over the noodles. Sprinkle with half of the cheddar cheese. Repeat the layering process.

5 On top, spread the cream of mushroom mixture and top with parmesan cheese. Bake for 35 minutes. ✎

—Betty Custer of Greenacres, WA, sent this recipe in. We think it would be perfect for a cold winter day.

Bean and Hamburger Casserole

INGREDIENTS:

1	lb. ground beef
1	onion, chopped
1	cup brown sugar
2	cups canned tomatoes
1	large can baked beans
½ to ¾	tsp. Chili Powder

1 Preheat oven to 325°.

2 Brown hamburger and onion.

3 Mix in the rest of ingredients and pour into a 9 x 13 pan.

4 Bake 1 hour. ✎

—Spokane's Bev Harthill sent in this casserole dish that is hardy and easy.

Mom's Casserole

INGREDIENTS:	
1	lb. ground beef
1	large onion, chopped
1	green onion, chopped
1	cup cooked spaghetti
½	can kidney beans (optional)
1	can mushrooms, drained
1	can diced, peeled tomatoes
6	slices of bacon, crumbled

1 Preheat oven to 350°.

2 Brown the beef slowly with the onion and green pepper. Add the cooked spaghetti, beans (if desired), mushrooms, tomatoes and bacon. Bake for 30-40 minutes. ∽

—Edith St. John sends this recipe from Tekoa, WA. Her mom used to make it and she has carried on the tradition. She sends it with her grandsons when they head out fishing.

Layered Zucchini Casserole

INGREDIENTS:	
1	lb. ground beef
1	onion, chopped
½	cup chopped green or red pepper
1½	slices dry bread, cubed
2-3	small zucchini, sliced
1	cup grated cheddar cheese
1	15 oz. can tomato sauce
	Salt and pepper

1 Preheat oven to 350°.

2 Brown beef, onion and pepper. Put half of the beef mixture into 2 qt. casserole dish. Arrange sliced zucchini over beef . Add salt and pepper. Put half of the cubed bread and half of the cheese over top. Repeat for two layers. Pour tomato sauce over the top. Cover and bake 1 hour. ∽

—Shirley Shaffer of Hayden, ID, sent this casserole dish. It may sound like a light side dish but don't be fooled. It's a meal!

One Dish Casserole

Kathy Wynia of Spokane sent this easy one-dish recipe in that takes just minutes to make.

§ Kathy sprinkles 1 lb. raw hamburger on the bottom of a 9 x 9 baking dish. Next she sprinkles 1 pkg. of dry onion soup mix over the meat. She then spreads 2 cups of frozen mixed vegetables on top of the dry soup. Kathy covers the mixture with 1 can cream of chicken soup (don't dilute the soup). Finally she tops with 1 pkg. of tater tots and bakes at 350° for 45 minutes to 1 hour. ∽

Quick Fix

Manicotti

INGREDIENTS:

1	lb. ground beef
1	clove garlic, minced
1	cup cottage cheese
4	oz. mozzarella, shredded
½	tsp. salt
½	cup mayonnaise
8	manicotti shells, partially cooked and drained
1	16 oz. jar of spaghetti sauce
½	tsp. oregano
	Parmesan cheese (to taste)

1 Preheat oven to 325°.

2 In skillet, brown meat and garlic. Drain fat.

3 In a bowl, blend cottage cheese, mozzarella, salt and mayonnaise. Add to meat mixture.

4 Fill shells with meat mixture. Place shells in a baking dish. Cover with remaining filling.

5 Top with spaghetti sauce, oregano and parmesan. Cover with foil and bake for 30 minutes at 325°. Uncover and bake for another 10 minutes. ∾

—Louise Bunn of Spokane sent in this recipe for manicotti. If you skip lunch you might have room to fit in this rich and delicious meal.

Better Than Barbecued Spareribs

INGREDIENTS:

5-6	lbs. country style spareribs (cut into serving size pieces)
	Water
1	cup prepared coffee
1	cup molasses
½	tsp. salt
⅓	cup mustard
1	Tbsp. Worcestershire sauce
⅓	cup cider vinegar
2-3	dashes of hot pepper sauce

1 Preheat oven to 350°.

2 Arrange spareribs 1 layer deep on a rack in a shallow roasting pan. Add water to cover bottom of pan.

3 Roast 1 hour. Pour drippings from the pan. Remove rack and place ribs in pan.

4 In a small saucepan, combine remaining ingredients. Stir over medium heat until blended and steaming. Pour over ribs. Bake 30 more minutes while basting frequently with sauce. ∾

—Caye Wademan sends this in from Spokane.

Turkey Florentine

INGREDIENTS:	
1	10 oz. frozen chopped spinach (partially thawed and drained)
2	cups cooked turkey, cubed
2	cups cooked rice (white or brown)
1	cup sour cream
⅓	cup grated parmesan or mozzarella cheese
¼	tsp. salt (optional)

1 Preheat oven to 350°.

2 Combine spinach, turkey, rice and sour cream. Place mixture into a baking dish and top with cheese.

3 Bake for 30 minutes. ∽

—Barrie MacConnell of Spokane has a great recipe to use up those Thanksgiving leftovers.

Newspeople always love a little 'Dish'

Turkey Enchiladas

INGREDIENTS:	
1	cup evaporated milk
1	8 oz. package cream cheese
1	can cream of chicken soup
1	tsp. garlic powder
4	cups cooked turkey, diced
1	cup black olives, sliced
1	cup monterey jack cheese, shredded
½	cup medium cheddar cheese, shredded
12	flour tortillas
	Salt

1 Preheat oven to 325°.

2 In a large pan heat evaporated milk, cream cheese, chicken soup, and garlic powder. Heat until bubbly.

3 Reduce the heat and add the turkey and olives. Combine well.

4 Put 3-4 Tbsp. of mixture into flour tortillas and roll up. Place enchiladas in 9 x 13 pan and pour remaining filling on top.

5 Top with cheeses and bake uncovered for 25 minutes. ∽

—Jean Anstadt of Spokane has a little twist in this enchilada recipe. Instead of the usual beef or chicken she slips in turkey.

Pork and Green Chili Casserole

	INGREDIENTS:
1½	lbs. boneless pork, cubed
1	Tbsp. vegetable oil
1	15 oz. can black beans, rinsed & drained
1	10¾ oz. can condensed cream of chicken soup, undiluted
1	14½ oz. can diced tomatoes, undrained
2	4 oz. cans chopped green chilies
1	cup uncooked instant brown rice
¼	cup water
2-3	Tbsp. salsa
1	tsp. ground cumin
½	cup shredded cheddar cheese

1 In a large skillet; sauté pork in oil until no pink remains. Drain skillet.

2 Add the beans, soup, tomatoes, chilies, rice, water, salsa, and cumin; cook and stir until bubbly.

3 Pour into an ungreased, 2 quart baking dish. Bake uncovered for 30 minutes at 350°. Dish should be bubbly. Sprinkle with cheese. Let stand for a few minutes before serving. ✺

—Mary Beth Junkin sent in this recipe. It's got just a little spice, but a whole lot of flavor!

Coffee Glazed Ham

	INGREDIENTS:
7	lb. ham (cooked)
½	cup brown sugar
¼	cup maple syrup
2	Tbsp. cider vinegar
1	Tbsp. Worcestershire sauce
1	Tbsp. instant coffee
1	Tbsp. dry mustard

1 Preheat oven to 350°.

2 Cut rind off the ham and expose fat. Place on rack and cover with foil. Bake 1 hour and 15 minutes.

3 While ham is baking, stir ingredients for glaze in a bowl until coffee dissolves. Brush liquid on ham.

4 Bake uncovered for 40-60 minutes basting twice with glaze. Let stand 15 minutes before serving (if you can wait that long!). ✺

—Barb Davis of Ephrata, WA, sent in this recipe that would be perfect for a holiday dinner (or a dinner worth celebrating)!

BBQ Pork on a Bun

	INGREDIENTS:
5	lb. pork roast
3	Tbsp. oil
	Garlic and salt to taste
2	cups water
1	14 oz. jar BBQ sauce
¾	cup brown sugar
2	tsp. liquid smoke

1 In a large pot, sear the meat on all sides. Sprinkle with garlic and salt. Place roast in a deep baking dish. Add water and cover tightly with foil. Bake for 4-5 hours at 300°. Allow 1 hour per pound baking time for any size roast. After 1 hour, check water level and add more if needed. Cover and reseal.

2 When baking time is up, remove meat from pan and cool. Take meat off bones and shred. Set aside.

3 In a bowl, mix BBQ sauce, brown sugar, and liquid smoke. Pour over meat and reheat.

4 Serve on hamburger buns. Watch out, it's messy! ∾

—Dee Woo of Pinehurst, ID, sends this recipe that would be perfect for a winter lunch. We talked to her Mom though and found out that Dee steals all the recipes from her!

Cajun Pork Chop Strips

	INGREDIENTS:
1	Tbsp. flour
1	tsp. poultry seasoning
¾	tsp. garlic salt
½	tsp. paprika
¼	tsp. black pepper
¼	tsp. cayenne pepper (or less according to taste)
1½	lbs. boneless pork chops, cut into strips
2	Tbsp. butter or margarine
	Italian parsley & chili peppers (optional)

1 In large resealable plastic bag; combine flour, poultry seasoning, garlic salt, paprika, and peppers. Add pork chops, shake and coat.

2 In a large skillet; cook pork strips in butter for 8-10 minutes or until juices run clear. ∾

—Jan Krepcik of Mead, WA, sent in this recipe for pork strips but she says you can use chicken if you want.

Pasta Sauce Supreme

INGREDIENTS:	
1	Tbsp. salad oil
2	links of mild Italian pork sausage
1	medium onion, chopped
¼	lb. lean ground beef
1	clove garlic, minced
1	carrot, finely chopped
¼	lb. mushrooms, sliced
1	stalk celery, chopped
2	lbs. canned tomatoes, broken up
1	6 oz. can tomato paste
½	cup dry red wine
1	tsp. basil leaves
⅛	tsp. rubbed sage
½	cup chopped parsley
½	tsp. salt
¼	tsp. pepper
	Pasta

1 Heat oil over medium heat in 3 qt. sauce pan. Squeeze sausage meat from casing and break up in oil. Brown the meat stirring occasionally.

2 Add onion and cook until translucent. Add ground beef and brown. Stir in garlic, carrot, mushrooms, and celery. Cook for two minutes. Drain fat.

3 Stir in tomatoes (broken), tomato paste, wine, basil, sage, parsley, salt and pepper.

4 Cover; simmer sauce for 2 hours on low heat. Sauce should thicken. Serve over hot pasta and pass around with grated cheese. ❧

—This recipe sent in from Ruth Stanley of Cheney, WA, takes some serious ingredients and time but it is well worth the effort. You can double the recipe and freeze the leftovers!

Pork Chop Casserole

INGREDIENTS:	
6	medium pork chops
1	can consommé beef broth
1	can water
1½	cups rice (raw)
½	tsp. dried parsley
1	Tbsp. dried onion bits
	Salt and pepper

In a casserole dish; mix broth, water, rice, parsley, and onion bits. Lay pork chops on top of mixture. Cover and bake for 45 minutes to 1 hour at 400°. ❧

—Marianna Rieg sends this recipe in from Hayden, ID. It's a great entertaining dish because it can be put together ahead of time.

Broiled Salmon

INGREDIENTS:	
½	cup olive oil
¼	cup light soy sauce
⅛	cup lemon juice (or one juicy lemon)
½	tsp. dill weed
	Pinch of ground clove
	Salmon steaks

1 Mix all the ingredients other than salmon steaks. Brush steaks with marinade. Place salmon marinade side down on an oiled baking sheet. Brush other side with marinade.

2 Broil salmon for 5 minutes. Turn salmon over. Brush again with marinade and broil for another 5 minutes or until lightly brown. Enjoy! ∾

—This is a quick an easy recipe that Charles loves to make when relaxing at home.

Charles Rowe anchors KREM 2 News weekday newscasts. He's been a member of the KREM 2 News team since 1987.

After growing up in Chadron, Nebraska, Charles proudly served in the U.S. Navy during the Korean War, attaining the rank of E6 in just 3 1/2 years. Following his honorable discharge, he attended Nebraska State at Chadron before embarking on his career as a journalist.

Over the years, Charles has been honored with a number of awards, winning four Emmys, a national Associated Press Award and 14 state awards while owner of K-Surf radio on the Oregon Coast. Charles loves the Inland Northwest and now calls Spokane home. He enjoys the relaxation of reading and photography.

Charles uses his favorite quote to put life and his job into perspective. "Good enough, never is."

Tyropitakia (Cheese Pies)

INGREDIENTS:

½	lb. feta cheese, crumbled
½	lb. ricotta cheese
½	lb. kasseri cheese, grated
¼	lb. cream cheese
½	lb. butter, melted
	Chopped parsley to taste
½	tsp. grated nutmeg
2	eggs, well-beaten
1	pkg. commercial phyllo pastry, thawed in refrigerator
½	tsp. white pepper

1 Preheat oven to 350°.

2 Combine all the cheese together with parsley, nutmeg, pepper and eggs. Mix well and chill in refrigerator for at least 1 hour.

3 Unroll phyllo dough. Hint: Make sure to keep the dough covered at all times with damp paper towels because it quickly dries out. Cut the phyllo dough into 4 strips.

4 One strip at a time, brush with melted butter and place a dollop of the cheese mixture in the middle and top of the strip.

5 Fold the right corner to the left, continue folding at right angles until you have one triangle. Place triangles on baking sheet. Bake for 20 minutes. ❧

—Jo Lynne Seufer says these cheese pies are fantastic fresh from the oven. By the way, these are not low-cal but they are good enough for you to blow off your diet at least for one meal!

Fettuccine Alfredo

INGREDIENTS:

1	lb. fettuccine
¼	cup butter (½ stick)
2	cups heavy cream
½	tsp. black pepper
1	cup grated parmesan cheese

1 Prepare the fettuccine according to the package directions, drain.

2 In a medium saucepan, melt the butter over medium-low heat and stir in cream and pepper. Cook for 8-10 minutes (until hot) stirring constantly. Stir in parmesan cheese until thoroughly combined. Cook for 3-5 minutes or until thickened. Stir frequently. Toss with pasta and serve. ❧

—Jenny Trainer sent this easy fettuccine recipe in from her kitchen in Spokane. It doesn't take long and it's worth every, single calorie.

Chili Relleno Casserole

INGREDIENTS:	
1	large can green chilies
1	lb. cheddar cheese
1	lb. jack cheese
1	13 oz. can condensed milk
1	tsp. salt
4	eggs, separated
3	Tbsp. flour
2	8 oz. cans tomato sauce

1 Preheat oven to 325°.

2 Split chilies and remove seeds. Grate cheeses but keep separate. Place a layer of chilies on the bottom of a baking dish. Cover with cheddar cheese. Put another layer of chilies and cover with jack cheese. Repeat layers until chilies and cheeses are gone.

3 In a small bowl beat egg yolks. Add milk, salt and flour. In a separate mixing bowl; beat egg whites until stiff. Fold egg whites into yolk mixture. Pour over chilies and cheeses.

4 Bake for 1 hour. Pour tomato sauce over top and bake for 30 more minutes. ❧

—*Maxine Congleton sent in this recipe.*

Portobello Mushroom Pasta

INGREDIENTS:	
1	cup fat-free chicken or vegetable broth
2	cloves garlic, minced
3	Tbsp. fat-free butter sprinkle
6	oz. portobello mushrooms
8	oz. pasta, cooked and drained (fettuccini or linguini)
1	red bell pepper, roasted and sliced
2	oz. feta cheese, crumbled

1 In large skillet, add garlic to ¾ cup of the broth. Add butter sprinkle and bring mixture to a boil.

2 Add mushrooms and cook over high heat until mushrooms are soft and liquid reduces by half.

3 Add pasta, remaining broth, and bell pepper to mushroom mixture. Stir until pasta is coated and liquid is warm. Sprinkle with cheese. ❧

—*Dawn Frederick of Spokane sent in this low-fat pasta dish. Low in fat, but high in taste!*

Barbecue

Tom Sherry's Chicken

INGREDIENTS:	
Chicken:	
4	large boneless, skinless chicken breasts
¼	cup soy sauce
2	Tbsp. vegetable oil
2	Tbsp. lemon juice
1	tsp. curry powder
1	tsp. toasted sesame oil
¼	tsp. ground coriander
1	garlic clove, minced
Peanut Sauce:	
4-5	Tbsp. hot water
¼	cup peanut butter
½	tsp. grated ginger root
⅛	tsp. crushed red pepper

▲ *When you think of weather here in the Inland Northwest you probably think of Tom Sherry (and Doppler the weather dog!). But Tom is more than just sunshine and snow…rain and wind.*

1 Rinse chicken and pat dry. Cut chicken lengthwise into one-inch wide strips. Place chicken strips in plastic bag.

◀ *Tom is a family man with a passion for helping others. Each year he helps collect thousands of turkeys for those in need during the holiday season with Tom's Turkey Drive. It's the largest turkey drive in the Inland Northwest. He also visits local schools (with Doppler in tow), hosts events, and dedicates himself to good causes like the Vanessa Behan Crisis Nursery and the Alzheimer's Association. When he does have some down time he spends it with his wife and two sons. Darlene, Michael (grey shirt), and Matthew (red shorts) are his real sunshine. They ski in the winter and boat and barbecue in the summer. Tom is the master of the grill! He does his BBQ forecast at KREM 2 and then feeds the whole newsroom (no wonder we love him). Happy grilling from Tom's family to yours.*

2 In a bowl combine soy sauce, oil, lemon juice, curry powder, sesame oil, coriander, and garlic. Pour mixture into plastic bag over chicken. Refrigerate for at least 2 hours.

3 To make peanut sauce; gradually stir hot water into peanut butter to create a smooth consistency. Stir in ginger root and red pepper.

4 Drain chicken and reserve marinade. Put chicken on skewers and grill over medium heat. Brush with reserved marinade about half-way through cooking. Cook until all pink is gone.

5 Serve chicken strips with peanut sauce. ∾

—Recipe submitted by Tom Sherry

Marinated Grilled Chicken

	INGREDIENTS:
4	skinless chicken breasts
	juice of ½ orange
	juice of 2 limes
¼	cup rice vinegar
¼	cup soy sauce
¼	cup olive oil
5	slices fresh ginger root
4	garlic cloves, minced
4	Tbsp. fresh cilantro
	pinch of sugar
	pinch of caraway seeds

Except for chicken, combine all ingredients in a large resealable plastic bag. Place chicken in bag and seal tightly. Marinate for 3-24 hours. Barbecue chicken and baste with marinade. Grill chicken until pink is gone. **(Remember, the marinade had raw chicken in it so make sure to stop basting about 10 minutes before chicken is cooked.)** ∾

—This recipe was sent by Diane Sampson. She cooks up some great chicken at her home in Lewiston, ID.

Chicken Marinade

Daryn Iltz of Ritzville, WA, likes to marinate his chicken in different salad dressings. He throws about 6-10 pieces of chicken into a resealable plastic bag and adds a bottle of his favorite dressing. He recommends using Italian, French, Russian, Orange, or Sesame dressing as a marinade. Let the bag of chicken sit in the refrigerator overnight and grill it the next day. ∾

Quick Fix

Beef and Bacon Shish Kabobs

	INGREDIENTS:
½	cup steak sauce
¼	cup dry sherry
2	Tbsp. honey
1	lb. boneless beef top sirloin, cubed
20	slices of bacon (about 1 pound)
1	large onion, cut into chunks
16	mushroom caps

1 In a bowl, mix steak sauce, sherry, and honey. Place steak cubes in the bowl. Cover and refrigerate for an hour, stirring occasionally. Meanwhile, cook bacon in a skillet until done, but not crisp. Drain bacon on paper towel.

2 Remove beef cubes from marinade. Wrap bacon around each steak cube. Put cubes on skewer alternating onions and mushrooms in between beef. Grill for 8-12 minutes or until desired doneness. ✎

—This recipe was sent in by Diane Barkley. It's a great recipe that all the family will love when grilling outdoors.

Burgers Cornucopia

	INGREDIENTS:
½	cup frozen corn
1½	lbs. ground beef
1	tsp. seasoned salt or seasoning
1	egg
½	cup cheddar cheese, grated
2	Tbsp. salsa

1 Boil the frozen corn in lightly salted water. Drain and refrigerate corn until chilled. Meanwhile, flavor ground beef with seasoned salt or seasoning. Stir egg into ground beef mixture until blended. Take corn out of refrigerator. Make sure it is well-drained. Add salsa and shredded cheese to corn.

2 Divide meat into 6-8 even portions. Flatten portions into round patties. Put a dollop of corn-cheddar relish in the middle of half the patties. Put the other patties on top to seal in the corn mixture. Grill until desired doneness. ✎

—This recipe was submitted by John Bonnier of Spokane.

Quick Fix

Alan's BBQ Asparagus

Colleen Adamek from Wenatchee, WA, sent in this simple recipe for grilled asparagus. It goes perfectly with any of the grilled meat dishes.

❧ Buy a large bundle of asparagus and a package of bacon. Take four stocks of asparagus and wrap in a slice of bacon. Try to cover as much of the asparagus as you can. Place asparagus on grill. Cook until bacon is crispy. Yum! ✎

BBQ Sauce

It seems like everyone has their favorite barbecue sauce recipe. Here's one from Jay Rea of Cheney, WA.

§ Jay pours 24-oz. catsup into a bowl. He then pours ½ cup white vinegar into the catsup bottle, shakes and then pours the vinegar into the bowl. Slowly add in ⅔ cup light brown sugar while whisking it into the catsup. Taste often until you get desired sweetness. Add 1 tsp. ground mustard and thoroughly mix. Now pour in ¼ cup Worcestershire sauce followed by 2 Tbsp. lemon juice concentrate. It creates a sweet and sour sauce. ∽

Grilled Lemon Basted Shish Kabobs

INGREDIENTS:	
Lemon Marinade and Baste:	
¼	cup lemon juice
2	Tbsp. vinegar
1	Tbsp. olive oil
½	tsp. garlic salt
½	tsp. onion powder
⅛	tsp. garlic powder
¼	tsp. parsley
	Dash Pepper
Kabob:	
1-2	lbs. top sirloin, cubed
1	green pepper, cut into 1 1/2 inch pieces
1	onion, quartered and separated
1	small zucchini, sliced into 1/4 inch rounds
¼	lb. mushroom caps
	Cherry tomatoes
	Pineapple chunks
2	Tbsp. olive oil

1 In a bowl, mix together ingredients for lemon marinade. Pour mixture over cubed meat and chill, covered, for at least 1 hour.

2 Combine vegetables and fruit in a large bowl and drizzle olive oil on top. Toss to coat.

3 Alternating, thread beef, vegetables, and fruit onto skewers.

4 Grill over medium heat while basting, until desired doneness. ∽

—Debbie Craig sent us this recipe.

Foil Grilled Roast

INGREDIENTS:	
4	lbs. pot roast
3	Tbsp. flour
1	Tbsp. brown sugar
1½	tsp. salt
½	tsp. pepper
½	tsp. dry mustard
¾	cup catsup
1½	Tbsp. Worcestershire sauce
1	Tbsp. vinegar

1 Brown roast slowly on grill for 20-30 minutes. In a bowl, combine flour, brown sugar, salt, pepper, and mustard. Stir in catsup, worcestershire, and vinegar.

2 Tear off a 4-foot piece of heavy-duty foil and fold in half. Spoon half of the sauce into the center of the foil. Place roast on top; cover with remaining sauce. Fold up foil to cover roast making sure to seal tightly. Place on grill about 5 inches from glowing coals. Cook for 2-2½ hours or until desired doneness. ❧

—Billie Hawks sent this recipe from Libby, MT.

Lemon Flank Steak

INGREDIENTS:	
1½	lb. flank steak, london broil, or tri-tip steaks
2	green onions, chopped
½	cup Italian salad dressing
2	Tbsp. lemon juice
¼	cup soy sauce
⅛	tsp. lemon pepper
¼	cup dry white wine
1	garlic clove, minced

1 In a bowl or large measuring cup combine onions, salad dressing, lemon juice, soy sauce, lemon pepper, wine, and garlic. Mix well.

2 Pour mixture over steak. Cover and refrigerate for at least 8 hours. Barbecue meat and brush with extra marinade while grilling. ❧

—This recipe was sent by Joyce Roden.

Quick Fix

Surprise Burgers

David Sylvester sent in this recipe to liven up burgers. He makes his burger patties about 3-4 inches in diameter and about 1 inch thick. After adding a little steak seasoning he puts garlic cloves or crystallized ginger into the middle of the burger. He covers up the garlic or ginger with a bit of meat before placing on the grill. He says people love the flavor burst when they bite into the middle! Serve with a side of raspberry chipolte sauce.

Applewood Smoked Ribs

INGREDIENTS:	
2	racks of baby back ribs
1	jar Woody's Smoke Sauce
1	small package of applewood chips
	sea salt
	ground pepper
	juice of one lemon
1	bottle of favorite barbeque sauce

1 Night before: brush the meaty side of the ribs with the smoke sauce. Use only about ⅓ of the jar. Salt and pepper the ribs.

2 Put ribs in the refrigerator for the night. Meanwhile, soak a handful of applewood chips in water. Let them sit overnight.

3 The next day, turn the gas grill on low on only one side. On the heated side, put a small pan of water to give the grill some moisture.

4 Put the marinated ribs on the other side of the grill over the indirect heat. Turn the ribs every couple of hours (for a total of 6-8 hours) and throw some soaked applewood chips over the low heat. Close the lid and let the smoke circulate.

5 In a small bowl, combine the barbeque sauce with the juice of one lemon. About 30 minute before you're ready to serve the ribs; turn on heat directly under the ribs to medium.

6 Every five minutes baste with barbecue sauce mixture. Watch closely or barbecue sauce can scorch. ∾

—Steve Haskell says he's been experimenting with ribs for over 20 years and this is his favorite recipe! He says the secret is time, moisture, and only a little bit of smoke.

Marinated Pork Tenderloin

INGREDIENTS:	
2	pork tenderloins (approx. ¾ lb. each)
1	1 inch piece of ginger, peeled and minced
1	jalapeno pepper, seeded and minced
¼	tsp. crushed red pepper flakes
⅓	cup honey
2	Tbsp. soy sauce
3	Tbsp. sesame oil

In a heavy resealable plastic bag; combine ginger, jalapeno, red pepper, honey, soy sauce, and sesame oil. Place tenderloins in the bag. (You can divide ingredients and do two separate bags if necessary) Let the meat marinate for a minimum of one hour to overnight. Reserve the marinade for basting. Grill over medium heat for approximately 10 minutes. Turn once and baste. Cook until desired doneness. ∾

—Patrice Preston from Mead, WA, admits she stole this recipe from her cousin. Fortunately, her cousin lives in Connecticut and will never know she let the secret out! We're glad Patrice spilled the beans.

Tasty Turkey Marinade

¾	cup orange juice
¾	cup soy sauce
¾	cup honey
4	garlic cloves, crushed
½	cup chopped green onion
2	tsp. black pepper
2	tsp. ground ginger
4	lbs. raw turkey

1 In a large bowl or baking dish, combine all ingredients except for turkey. Mix well. Add turkey to mixture; cover and refrigerate. Let turkey marinate for an hour.

2 Grill turkey until all pink is gone. Discard leftover marinade that is not used for basting. ❧

—Alberta Rice of Spokane sent in this recipe. Perfect for a summer night of grilling!

Al's Favorite Fish

1	salmon filet, skinned (Sockeye or Coho salmon)
1	Tbsp. olive oil
4	cloves garlic, chopped
2	Tbsp. capers
⅓	cup olives, cut into rings
	Italian breadcrumbs

1 Rub one side of fish with olive oil. Spread the same side with garlic. Top with capers and olives. Cover top with a thin layer of breadcrumbs. Place fish on thick layer of tin foil. Place on grill and cook until fish is done. Time is dependent on size and thickness of fish. Check often and cook until flaky.

2 Place fish on baking sheet. Place under hot broiler until breadcrumbs are crispy. Broiler will only take a moment. Watch closely as to not burn. ❧

—Al Lozano is a KREM 2 photojournalist and a master at the grill.

Quick Fix

Fresh Cranberry Relish

Dorothy de Vica sent in this recipe for a fresh cranberry relish to go along with some of your main dishes.

❧ Wash, core, and seed; two apples, two oranges, and one lemon. Combine the fruit and grind. In a separate large bowl, grind 1 12oz. pkg. of frozen cranberries. Add cranberries to other fruit. Now add 1 can crushed pineapple (juice included), and 2 cups of sugar. Mix well and refrigerate for 2 days. Occasionally stir. Serve on the side with poultry. Goes well with all meats. Perfect with sandwiches. ❧

Barbecue Tip

When grilling ribs on a gas grill: First sear the ribs. Then cook them indirectly by turning off one of the burners and placing the ribs over it. Keep the other burner on medium and close the lid. Most ribs will be ready in 60 to 90 minutes. During the last 15 minutes of cooking, apply the BBQ sauce. Be careful it doesn't burn. ∾

BBQ Sauce

INGREDIENTS:	
2	Tbsp. brown sugar
1	Tbsp. paprika
1	Tbsp. salt
1	tsp. dry mustard
2	Tbsp. Worcestershire sauce
1	cup tomato juice
¼	cup catsup
½	cup water
¼	tsp. chili powder
⅛	tsp. cayenne pepper
¼	cup vinegar

To make the sauce; simmer ingredients for 15-minutes. You can pour the sauce over your favorite meats while grilling. ∾

—This sauce recipe was sent in by Kay Cotant of Greenacres, WA. She received the recipe at her bridal shower 34 years ago.

Sharon's Favorite BBQ Sauce

INGREDIENTS:	
½	cup cider vinegar
1	cup brown sugar
1	can tomato puree
1	tsp. cumin
1	tsp. granulated garlic
1	tsp. sea salt
1	tsp. five spice
½	cup water

In a saucepan, combine all ingredients and stir well. Cook over medium heat for 10-15 minutes. Use immediately on chicken, beef, or pork. ∾

—Everyone has their favorite sauce! This one was sent in by Sharon Sokoll of Addy, WA.

Desserts

▲ *Tom Hudson is KREM 2's Sports Director and the Voice of the Zags. He hails from Texas but he enjoys everything the Northwest has to offer.*

Key Lime Pie

INGREDIENTS:	
1	small can Eagle Brand condensed milk
1	small can frozen limeade
1	carton Cool Whip
1	lime (juice and garnish)
1	graham cracker crust
	Green food coloring (optional)

1 Mix milk and limeade. Fold in a little more than half the Cool Whip. (Reserve enough to top pie). Add extra lime juice if desired. Add food coloring if desired.

2 Pour mixture into pie shell.

3 Top with Cool Whip. Refrigerate.

4 Slice lime thin, then twist to garnish top of pie. ∾

—*Recipe submitted by Tom and Kate Hudson.*

◀ *Tom and his wife Kate (a KREM 2 producer) spend their time with Fielder (the cutest American Water Spaniel you've ever seen). Tom doesn't just love to report sports, he also plays them. He's an avid golfer. Tom and Kate also spend a lot of time fixing up their 1925 home and traveling to see family in Texas (Tom) and Alaska (Kate). Tom always serves up a 'sweet' sportscast.*

Desserts

Toffee Macadamia Nut Delights

INGREDIENTS:

1½	cups unsalted butter, room temperature
1	cup sugar
¾	cup light brown sugar, packed
2	large eggs
1	tsp. vanilla
4	cups flour
2	tsp. baking soda
1	tsp. salt
3	cups toffee chips
2½	cups macadamia nuts, coarsely chopped

1 Preheat oven to 350°.

2 In a bowl, beat butter and sugars on medium speed until light and fluffy (about 2 minutes). Add eggs and vanilla extract. Beat until well mixed.

3 In a separate bowl, whisk flour, baking soda, and salt together. Add to butter mixture. Stir in toffee chips and nuts.

4 Place spoonfuls of dough onto cookie sheet about two inches apart. Flatten cookies slightly with glass or hand. Bake about 10-15 minutes. ✎

—Weekend and Noon Anchor Kristi Gorenson makes these special cookies for the newsroom. They are inhaled so fast sometimes you're not even sure they were there. You gotta be fast!

Kristi Gorenson co-anchors the Weekend Edition (with Sten Walstrom) and anchors KREM 2 News at Noon. She and her husband Dan love to cook dinner together. On special days she brings us some of her amazing toffee chip cookies for a sweet treat. Kristi is a Washington native. She grew up in Puyallup and graduated from Washington State University. Go Cougs! When she's not telling us the news, she loves spending time with her family. Who wouldn't love spending time with the sweetest of little girls, Haley.

Pineapple Cookies

INGREDIENTS:

1	cup soft shortening
1⅓	cup sugar
1	egg
1	9 oz. can crushed pineapple
4	cups flour
1	tsp. baking soda
½	tsp. salt
½	cup nuts (optional)

1 Preheat oven to 400°.

2 Thoroughly mix shortening, sugar and egg. Stir in pineapple, flour, baking soda, and salt.

3 Chill mixture at least 1 hour.

4 Drop by spoonful on a baking sheet coated with non-stick spray. Bake for 10 minutes. ❧

—Ilene Greenwood of Spokane sent in this recipe that she often makes for church. The cookies are soft and chewy (and a bit addictive!).

Margaret's Oatmeal Cookies

INGREDIENTS:

1½	cups brown sugar
1	cup shortening
2	eggs
1	tsp. vanilla
1	tsp. baking soda
¼	cup boiling water
2	cups quick oats
1½	cups flour
1	tsp. salt
1	cup chopped nuts (optional)
1⅓	cup chocolate chips

1 Preheat oven to 350°.

2 Cream together brown sugar and shortening. Add eggs and vanilla.

3 In a separate bowl; mix the baking soda with the boiling water. Add baking soda mixture into the brown sugar mixture. Add oats, flour, salt and nuts. Add chocolate chips if desired.

4 Drop by the spoonful on an ungreased cookie sheet. Bake for 10 minutes. Cool on racks. ❧

—Carol MacPherson of Spokane sent in her favorite version of the oatmeal cookie created by her Aunt Margaret. It could become your favorite as well.

Filled Oatmeal Cookies

INGREDIENTS:

Cookie:
1	cup shortening
1	cup sugar
1	tsp. baking soda
½	cup warm water
2½	cups oatmeal
2½	cups flour
1-2	tsp. nutmeg

Filling:
½	lb. raisins
1	cup water
2½	cups sugar

1 Preheat oven to 350°.

2 In a small bowl, dissolve baking soda into ½ cup warm water. In a large bowl, mix together all the ingredients for the cookie. Add baking soda mixture. Roll thin and cut with any size cookie cutter. Bake for 8-10 minutes. Cookies should just be turning light brown. Take out and cool. Set aside.

3 Meanwhile, to prepare filling, mix raisins, water, and sugar in a saucepan. Cook on medium heat until mixed and heated through. Cool. Spread filling between two cookies. ∾

—Spokane viewer Ada Mae Scott submitted her Grandmother's recipe. We're glad she shared.

Chocolate Cottage Cheese Cookies

INGREDIENTS:

3½	cups sugar
1⅓	cup shortening
4	eggs
4	tsp. vanilla
1	pint cottage cheese
½	cup baking cocoa
6	cups flour
2	tsp. baking powder
1½	tsp. salt
1	cup nuts (optional)
	Powdered sugar

1 Preheat oven to 325°.

2 In large bowl, mix together sugar, shortening, eggs and vanilla. Add cottage cheese and baking cocoa. Mix well. Add flour, baking powder, and salt. Stir. Add nuts (if desired).

3 Form spoonfuls of cookie dough into balls. Roll into powdered sugar. Set on greased cookie sheet and flatten slightly with a spatula. Bake for 10-12 minutes. ∾

—In Silverton, ID, Sue Pollard bakes up batches of these cookies. Now you can as well!

Banana Oatmeal Cookies

INGREDIENTS:

¾	cup butter
1	cup sugar
1	egg
1	cup mashed bananas
1½	cups quick cooking oats
1	tsp. vanilla
½	cup nutmeats (shelled nuts)
1½	cup flour
1	tsp. salt
½	tsp. baking soda
½	tsp. nutmeg
¾	tsp. cinnamon
	Frosting (optional)

1 Preheat oven to 400°.

2 Cream together butter and sugar. Add the egg, bananas, oats, vanilla, and nutmeats. Mix well and add flour, salt, baking soda, nutmeg, and cinnamon.

3 Drop spoonfuls on a greased cookie sheet. Bake for 10-12 minutes. Cool. Add frosting if desired. ∾

—Adeline Hardin from Spokane developed this recipe that gives oatmeal cookies a kick with a little banana.

Amish Sugar Cookies

INGREDIENTS:

1	cup butter or margarine
1	cup vegetable oil
1	cup sugar
1	cup powdered sugar
2	large eggs
1	tsp. vanilla
4½	cups flour
1	tsp. baking soda
1	tsp. cream of tartar

1 Preheat oven to 375°.

2 In bowl, combine butter, oil, both sugars and eggs. Beat until blended. Add vanilla.

3 In separate bowl, combine flour, baking soda and cream of tartar. Add dry ingredients to creamed mixture.

4 Take a spoonful of mixture and mold into ball. Drop onto ungreased baking sheet. Bake for 12-15 minutes. ∾

—Helen Reed of Spokane sent in this recipe. They're perfect for the holidays (or really any day).

Non-Dairy Sugar Cookies

INGREDIENTS:

4	cups flour
1½	cups sugar
2	tsp. baking powder
1	tsp. baking soda
1	tsp. salt
1	cup shortening or butter
2	eggs
⅔	cup Mocha Mix non-dairy milk
1½	tsp. vanilla (or other flavorings such as lemon or almond)

1 Preheat oven to 350°.

2 Mix flour, sugar, baking powder, baking soda, and salt. With a fork, cut in shortening or butter. In a separate bowl, mix eggs, non-dairy milk, and vanilla. Add egg mixture to dry ingredients. Roll out dough and cut with cookie-cutters. Place on ungreased cookie sheet and bake for 8-10 minutes. ❧

—Vonnie Lowther sent in this recipe for Hayden, ID.

Oatmeal Snap Cookies

INGREDIENTS:

1½	cups shortening
2	cups sugar
½	cup molasses (light or dark)
2	eggs, beaten
2⅔	cups flour
2	cups oatmeal
½	tsp. salt
4	tsp. baking soda
2	tsp. cinnamon
2	tsp. cloves
2	tsp. ginger

1 Mix shortening, sugar, eggs, and molasses. Add dry ingredients.

2 Shape into balls about the size of a walnut and place on ungreased cookie sheets. Bake for 10-12 minutes at 350°. ❧

—Spokane's Anne Michels sent in this recipe with cinnamon, cloves, and ginger that gives the cookie a little extra 'snap'.

Choco-Scotch Clusters

Velma Weisgerber of Spokane sent in this easy no-bake recipe.

❧ In heavy saucepan over low heat, melt 6 oz. chocolate chips, 6 oz. butterscotch chips, and ¼ cup peanut butter . Add 4 cups of Rice Krispies and stir until well coated. Drop by teaspoon onto waxed paper. Cool. ❧

Quick Fix

No Bake Peanut Butter Cookies

INGREDIENTS:

1	cup margarine
4	cups sugar
1	cup milk
1	tsp. salt
1	cup peanut butter
1	tsp. vanilla
5	cups rolled oats

1 Mix margarine, sugar, milk, and salt in a saucepan. Bring to a boil for 10 minutes.

2 Remove from heat. Add peanut butter, vanilla and oats. Mix well.

3 Drop by spoonfuls on cookie sheet or wax paper. Let sit until firm. ❧

—There's no baking in these cookies but a whole lot of taste. The recipe was sent in by Elsie Voll of Bonners Ferry, ID.

Pecan Crunch Cookies

INGREDIENTS:

1	cup butter
½	cup sugar
1	tsp. vanilla
½	cup crushed potato chips
½	cup pecans, chopped
2	cups flour, sifted

1 Cream together butter, sugar and vanilla. Add potato chips, pecans and flour.

2 Form dough into small balls and place on an ungreased cookie sheet. Press flat with a glass or meat-tenderizer.

3 Bake 15-18 minutes in a 350° oven. ❧

—Nelma Johnson sent in this recipe from her Spokane kitchen. A cookie that has potato chips in the recipe! Yum!

Quick Fix

Peanut Butter Cookies

You have to love a cookie with only four ingredients and big taste. This peanut butter cookie recipe sent in by Doris Cook of Walla Walla, doesn't use any flour.

§ Mix together 1 cup of peanut butter, 1 cup of sugar, 1 egg, and 1 teaspoon of vanilla. Place on cookie sheet and bake for 8-10 minutes at 350°. ❧

Fresh Orange Cookies

INGREDIENTS:

Cookie:

1½	cups sugar
1	cup margarine or butter, softened
1	cup sour cream
2	eggs
4	cups flour
1	tsp. baking soda
1	tsp. baking powder
½	tsp. salt
⅔	cup orange juice
3	Tbsp. grated orange peel

Frosting:

¼	cup margarine or butter, melted
2	cups powdered sugar
1	Tbsp. grated orange peel
2-3	Tbsp. orange juice

1 Preheat oven to 375°.

2 In large bowl, cream sugar and margarine until fluffy. Add sour cream and eggs. Blend well.

3 Lightly spoon flour into measuring cup and level off. Add flour, baking soda, baking powder, salt, orange juice and orange peel. Mix well.

4 Drop by rounded teaspoons onto ungreased cookie sheet. Bake for 8-11 minutes.

5 In small bowl, combine frosting ingredients. Beat until smooth. Frost slightly warm cookies. ∾

—Elaine Church of Sandpoint, ID, sent us this recipe for orange cookies. Perfect for a summer picnic.

Wheaties Cookies

INGREDIENTS:

½	cup applesauce
1	cup white sugar
1	cup brown sugar
2	eggs
1	tsp. baking soda
1	tsp. baking powder
½	tsp. salt
2	cups coconut
2	cups Wheaties
2	cups flour

1 Preheat oven to 375°.

2 Cream applesauce, sugars, and eggs. Add dry ingredients. Roll into balls and place on cookie sheet. Flatten cookies slightly with a fork. Bake for 10 minutes. ∾

—Edith (Edee) Bradley sent in this recipe from her Spokane kitchen. We're grateful she did!

Pumpkin Cookies

INGREDIENTS:

1	cup brown sugar
½	cup shortening
1	cup canned pumpkin
¼	cup white sugar
2	eggs
1½	cups flour
1	tsp. baking soda
1	tsp. ginger
1	tsp. cinnamon
	Salt
1	tsp. vanilla
½	pkg. of chocolate chips

1 Preheat oven to 350°.

2 Cream together sugars and shortening. Add pumpkin and mix well. Beat in eggs until well blended.

3 Add flour, baking soda, ginger, cinnamon and a dash of salt. Stir in vanilla and chocolate chips.

4 Drop by teaspoon on ungreased cookie sheet. Bake for 10-12 minutes. Frost with your favorite frosting, if desired! ❧

—Sharon Moskiland of Colville, WA, usually doubles this recipe because her family and friends love it so much.

'No Sugar' Applesauce-Raisin Drops

INGREDIENTS:

½	cup margarine, softened
⅓	cup brown sugar substitute
1	egg
1	cup flour
1¾	cup quick oats
1½	tsp. baking powder
½	tsp. baking soda
¾	tsp. cinnamon
¼	tsp. nutmeg
⅛	tsp. cloves
⅛	tsp. cream of tartar
1½	cups unsweetened applesauce
1½	tsp. vanilla
1	cup raisins

1 Preheat oven to 375°.

2 In large bowl, cream margarine until fluffy. Blend in brown sugar substitute and egg. Alternately add dry ingredients and applesauce. Blend well. Stir in vanilla and raisins.

3 Drop by the spoonful onto greased cookie sheet. Flatten slightly. Bake for 12-15 minutes. ❧

—Faith Franck of Thompson Falls, MT, makes these sugar-free cookies for her diabetic grandson and friends. We think even sugar lovers will like them.

Frosted Pumpkin Bars

INGREDIENTS:

Bars:

4	eggs, beaten
1	cup vegetable oil
2	cups sugar
1	cup canned pumpkin
½	tsp. salt
2	tsp. cinnamon
1	tsp. baking soda
1	tsp. baking powder
2	cups flour
1	cup raisins or nuts

Frosting:

3	oz. cream cheese
6	Tbsp. butter
¾	lb. powdered sugar
1	tsp. vanilla
1	tsp. milk

1 Combine all ingredients for bars. Grease and flour one large cookie sheet (or two smaller ones). Spread bar mixture onto cookie sheet. Bake for 20-25 minutes at 350°.

2 Meanwhile, combine cream cheese, butter, powdered sugar, vanilla and milk. Spread frosting on warm bars. Cut out of pan and eat! ∞

—Gertrude McFarland of Clarkston, WA, sent this recipe in for pumpkin bars. A perfect snack on a beautiful fall day.

Keysha Kay Bars

INGREDIENTS:

1	cup sugar
1	cup light corn syrup
1	cup peanut butter (creamy or chunky)
6	cups Rice Krispies
1	cup chocolate chips (optional)

1 In large kettle, cook sugar and corn syrup over medium heat until hot. Stir in peanut butter and cereal. Mix well.

2 Press into a 13 x 9 pan. While warm sprinkle with chocolate chips. Cool and cut out squares. ∞

—Constance Jack sent in this recipe from her kitchen in Spokane.

Special K Bars

Mildred Converse of Hayden, ID, has a similar recipe to the Keysha Kay Bars but uses Special K cereal instead of Rice Krispies.

§ Together, boil ¾ cup Karo Syrup and ¾ cup sugar. Remove from stove. Add 3 cups of Special 'K' cereal and 1 cup of peanut butter. Press into a 9 x 13 pan. Melt 6 oz. of chocolate chips with 6 oz. of butterscotch chips. Pour on top of cookie mixture. Cool and cut into squares. ∞

Quick Fix

Oatmeal Bars

	INGREDIENTS:
1	cup butter
2	cups brown sugar
2	eggs
1	Tbsp. vanilla
2½	cups flour
3	cups oats
1	tsp. baking soda
1	can sweetened condensed milk
12	oz. semi-sweet chocolate chips
¼	cup cocoa

1 In a saucepan, melt butter and mix with sugar, eggs and vanilla. In a separate bowl, mix flour, oats and baking soda. Add dry ingredients to the butter mixture.

2 Put 2/3 of the mixture in the bottom of a buttered 13 x 9 baking pan. Press down. Reserve the rest of the oat mixture.

3 In a saucepan, mix condensed milk, chocolate chips, and cocoa until well blended. Pour over the oat mixture.

4 Take reserved oat mixture and press on top of chocolate. Bake for 35 minutes at 350°. ∾

—This recipe was sent in from Ed Weilep who lives in the Spokane Valley.

Lemon Squares

	INGREDIENTS:
1	cup flour
½	cup butter or margarine, softened
¼	cup powdered sugar
1	cup sugar
2	tsp. grated lemon peel
2	Tbsp. lemon juice
½	tsp. baking powder
¼	tsp. salt
2	eggs

1 Preheat oven to 350°.

2 Thoroughly mix flour, butter, and powdered sugar. Press mixture evenly into the bottom of an ungreased 8 x 8 baking dish. Bake for 20 minutes.

3 Meanwhile, in a separate bowl beat sugar, lemon peel, lemon juice baking powder, salt, and eggs on medium speed until light and fluffy. Pour over hot crust.

4 Bake about 25 minutes (until no indentation remains when center is touched). Let stand until cool. Cut into 1½ inch squares. ∾

—Emily is 13-years-old and sent in this recipe. The lemon treat is sure to please your friends, if you feel like sharing.

Rhubarb Bars

INGREDIENTS:

Crust:
2	cups flour
¼	cup sugar
1	cup cold butter or margarine

Filling:
2	cups sugar
7	Tbsp. flour
1	cup whipping cream
3	eggs, beaten
5	cups finely chopped rhubarb (if frozen, thawed and drained)

Topping:
2-3	pkgs. (3 oz. each) cream cheese, softened
½	cup sugar
½	tsp. vanilla
1	cup whipping cream, whipped

1 Preheat oven to 350°.

2 In a bowl, combine flour and sugar. Cut in butter until mixture resembles course crumbs. Press into a greased 13 x 9 baking pan. Bake for 10 minutes. Remove from oven.

3 Meanwhile, combine sugar and flour in a bowl. Whisk in cream (not whipped) and eggs. Stir in rhubarb. Pour over crust. Bake for 40-45 minutes or until custard is set. Cool.

4 In mixing bowl, beat cream cheese, sugar, and vanilla until smooth; fold in whipped cream. Spread over top of cooled custard. Cover and chill. Cut into bars and store in refrigerator. ❧

—Kitty Bullinger of Davenport, WA, says this recipe is the best rhubarb concoction she's ever made. You may agree!

Pudding Bars

Elsie Voll of Bonners Ferry, ID, sent in this recipe for pudding bars.

❦ Prepare a box of any flavored instant pudding according to directions. Add one box of chocolate cake mix and a bag of chocolate chips. Mix well. Pour onto a greased cookie sheet and bake for 30-35 minutes at 350°. ❧

Toffee Bars

INGREDIENTS:

Bars:

⅔	cup melted butter or margarine
4	cups quick oats
1	cup brown sugar
½	cup corn syrup
1	tsp. salt
2	tsp. vanilla
¼	cup peanut butter

Topping:

1	6 oz. pkg. milk chocolate chips
¼	cup butterscotch chips
⅔	cup peanut butter
	Chopped nuts

1 In a bowl, mix melted butter to quick oats. Add the brown sugar, corn syrup, salt, vanilla, and peanut butter. Put in greased 9 x 13 pan and bake for 12 minutes at 400° degrees.

2 Melt chocolate chips along with butterscotch chips, and peanut butter. Spread over baked crust. Put chopped nuts on top and refrigerate. Cut in small squares because it is very rich. ∽

—Barbara Pedersen of Othello, WA, sent in this recipe for toffee bars. She likes to serve them with coffee on Sunday after church. Warning! You'll want to eat them 7-days a week.

Cherry Cheese Pie with Rice Krispie Crust

INGREDIENTS:

Pie Filling:

1	8 oz. cream cheese, softened
1	14 oz. sweetened condensed milk
⅓	cup Real Lemon juice
1	tsp. vanilla
1	21 oz. can of pie cherry filling

Crust:

¼	cup corn syrup
2	Tbsp. sugar
1	Tbsp. butter
3	cups Rice Krispies
	Whipped cream

1 Beat cream cheese until fluffy. Add sweetened condensed milk and beat until smooth. Add lemon juice and vanilla.

2 For crust, combine corn syrup, sugar, and butter in a saucepan. Cook over low heat stirring occasionally until bubbles begin to form. Remove from heat. Stir in Rice Krispies until well-coated. Press mixture into buttered 9-inch pie pan. Cover the bottom and sides of pan.

3 Pour cream cheese mixture into pie crust and chill at least 3 hours. Top with cherry pie filling and garnish with whipped cream. ∽

—Bee Rife from Silverton, ID, sends this recipe in that is a perfect summer treat.

Marshmallow Pie

INGREDIENTS:

½	lb. marshmallows
1	cup whipping cream
½	cup milk
1	sq. chocolate, shaved
1	pie shell crust, pre-cooked
	Whipping cream, garnish

1 Shave chocolate and set aside. In double boiler, cook marshmallows and milk until marshmallows dissolve. Set mixture in ice water bath to cool.

2 In separate bowl, beat whipping cream and add shaved chocolate. Blend in marshmallow mixture. Pour into pre-cooked pie shell. Chill 3-4 hours. Garnish with whipping cream and a little shaved chocolate. ✎

—Anna Henry of Cheney, WA, says this recipe is a 'winner'. She says you'll want this instead of birthday cake. Light up those candles and lets eat!

Peanut Butter Cream Pie

INGREDIENTS:

1	cup peanut butter
1	8 oz. pkg. cream cheese
1	cup sugar
2	Tbsp. melted margarine
1	Tbsp. vanilla
1	cup cream, whipped
	(any whipped topping will do)
	Graham cracker or chocolate crust
	Hot fudge topping

1 Cream together peanut butter, cream cheese, sugar, and margarine. Fold in cream and vanilla.

2 Pour into crust. Chill 6-8 hours. Top with melted hot fudge topping (thinned out a bit). Chill again for 30 minutes. ✎

—Mrs. Albert Kjack of Spokane sent in this no-bake recipe. Buy a store bought crust and this recipe only takes minutes, but you'll likely want seconds.

Lemonade Pie

Here's an easy pie sent in by Doni Grossarth of Thompson Falls, MT. It's a refreshing treat on a hot day!

§ Doni mixes 2 15 oz. cans of sweetened condensed milk, 1 12 oz. can of thawed frozen lemonade, and 2 small tubs of Cool Whip. She takes the mixture and pours it into 2 graham cracker crusts. Freeze or chill and you have a great dessert. You can add yellow or red food coloring to brighten the pie for special occasions (red would be perfect for July 4th celebrations!). ✎

Quick Fix

Little Pecan Pies

INGREDIENTS:

Crust:

1	3 oz. pkg. cream cheese
1	cup flour
1	stick (½ cup) butter or margarine

Filling:

¾	cup brown sugar
1	egg
¾	cup chopped pecans
1	Tbsp. butter or margarine
1	tsp. vanilla

1 Preheat oven to 350°.

2 For crust, mix cream cheese, flour, and butter together. Roll into 24 balls. Press balls into mini-muffin tins.

3 For filling, mix together sugar, egg, pecans, butter, and vanilla. Divide mixture into the muffin tins. Bake for 30 minutes. ❧

—Margaret Gray of Spokane submitted this mini-pie recipe that would be perfect for a holiday party. Careful, they're so good you may not share any with your guests.

Mile High Strawberry Pie

INGREDIENTS:

2	egg whites
1	Tbsp. lemon juice
1	cup sugar
1	10 oz. pkg. frozen strawberries
1	cup whipping cream, whipped
	Graham cracker crust
1	tsp. vanilla

1 Put ingredients (except vanilla and whipped cream) in large bowl and beat on high speed for 15 minutes.

2 Fold in whipping cream. Add vanilla. Pour into graham cracker crust and freeze for 3-4 hours. ❧

—Velma Dehmel sends this recipe from her kitchen in Moses Lake, WA. Buy a graham cracker crust and you won't have to bake a thing! Perfect for summer.

Sweet endings
from the set

Pumpkin Cake Roll

INGREDIENTS:

Cake:

3	eggs
1	cup sugar
⅔	cup canned pumpkin
1	tsp. lemon juice
¾	cup flour
1	tsp. baking powder
2	tsp. cinnamon
1	tsp. ginger
½	tsp. nutmeg
½	tsp. salt
	Powdered sugar

Filling:

1	cup powdered sugar
1	8 oz. cream cheese
4	Tbsp. margarine
½	tsp. vanilla

1 Preheat oven to 350°.

2 Beat eggs at high speed for 5 minutes. Beat in sugar, pumpkin, and lemon juice.

3 In a separate bowl, combine flour, baking powder, cinnamon, ginger, nutmeg, and salt. Fold dry ingredients into pumpkin mixture. Spread onto a greased and floured 1 x 15 x 10 pan. Bake for 15-20 minutes. Take out of oven and turn onto a towel. Sprinkle with powdered sugar. Roll up in towel and let cool.

4 For the filling; combine powdered sugar, cream cheese, margarine and vanilla. Beat ingredients until smooth. Spread on cooled cake. Roll up (beginning with longer edge) and cover in plastic wrap or foil. Place in refrigerator until well chilled. Slice and enjoy. ❧

—Marion Baskin of Brewster, WA, sent in this amazing recipe for a pumpkin roll.

Apple Cake

INGREDIENTS:

1	cup sugar
¼	cup butter or margarine
1	egg
1	tsp. cinnamon
1	tsp. vanilla
1	tsp. baking soda
	Pinch of salt
1	cup flour
2	cups apples, chopped and peeled
½	cup nuts, chopped

Preheat oven to 350°. Cream together sugar, butter, and egg. Stir in cinnamon, vanilla, baking soda, salt, and flour. Add apples and nuts. Stir. Pour into greased 8 x 8 pan. Bake for 35 minutes. ❧

—Lila Wieber of Spokane sent in her version of apple cake. It may very well become your version.

Zucchini Cake

INGREDIENTS:

1	cup white sugar
1	cup brown sugar
1	cup butter (no substitutes)
3	eggs
1	tsp. salt
½	tsp. baking powder
1	tsp. baking soda
2	tsp. cinnamon
3	tsp. vanilla
3	cups flour
2	cups shredded zucchini
1	pkg. cinnamon chips

1 Preheat oven to 325°.

2 You will need two smaller bundt pans for this recipe.

3 In a mixing bowl, beat sugars, butter, and eggs. Combine with salt, baking powder, baking soda, cinnamon, and vanilla. Add flour and zucchini while alternating between the two ingredients. Mix thoroughly. Add cinnamon chips.

4 Pour into two prepared bundt pans. Bake for 1 hour. Let sit for 5 minutes before removing cakes from pans. ❧

—Kay Kalidja of Hayden, ID, sends in this recipe. It's made with a vegetable, but it's all cake!

Grandma's Christmas Cake

INGREDIENTS:

1	cup chopped dates
1	tsp. baking soda
1	cup boiling water
¾	cup brown sugar
1	Tbsp. shortening
1	egg
1½	cups flour
¼	tsp. salt
¾	tsp. cinnamon
½	tsp. cloves
½	tsp. nutmeg
1	Tbsp. grated orange rind
1	cup raisins (optional)
½	cups chopped walnuts
1	cup gum drops, cut into small pieces

1 Preheat oven to 325°.

2 Sprinkle dates with baking soda and cover with boiling water. Let stand for a few minutes. Meanwhile, blend sugar, shortening, and egg. Combine the dates to the shortening mixture. Stir well. Add flour, salt, cinnamon, cloves, nutmeg, orange rind, raisins, walnuts, and gum drops. Pour mixture into a greased and floured bread pan (medium size). Bake for 1 hour. ❧

—This recipe was sent in by Beverly Dobbs of Spokane. She says her dad didn't like fruit cake so her mom came up with this recipe. If you want your house to smell like Christmas, just bake this cake.

Tomato Soup Cake

INGREDIENTS:

1	cup sugar
½	cup shortening
1	can tomato soup, not diluted*
2	eggs
1	cup raisins
1	cup chopped nuts, floured
2	cups flour
1	tsp. salt
2	tsp. baking powder
1	tsp. baking soda
1	tsp. cinnamon
1	tsp. nutmeg
½	tsp. ground cloves

* *(You can substitute soup with 1-15 oz. can of solid packed canned pumpkin)*

1 Preheat oven to 375°.

2 Cream together sugar and shortening. Add eggs and mix well. Add tomato soup and stir. Gradually add dry ingredients. Stir in flour coated nuts and raisins. Bake in a greased and floured bundt pan for 45-50 minutes. ❧

—This recipe comes from the kitchen of Ruth Anderson. Ruth is from Spokane. The cake may sound strange (tomato soup???) but who cares! It tastes fabulous.

Mini-Cheese Cakes

INGREDIENTS:

12	vanilla wafers
2	8 oz pkg. cream cheese
1	tsp. vanilla
½	cup sugar
2	eggs
1	can pie filling (any kind)
1	cup walnuts
	Shredded coconut

1 Preheat oven to 325°.

2 Line a muffin pan with cupcake liners. In each liner place one wafer. In a mixing bowl, beat cream cheese, vanilla, and sugar on medium speed. Once blended, add eggs.

3 Pour mixture into muffin tin liners. Fill each cup about three-fourths of the way. Bake for 25-30 minutes. Cool. Pour a bit of pie filling over cakes and top with nuts and coconut. Chill in refrigerator for several hours. ❧

—This recipe was sent in by Sandy Ponozzo of Spokane. They may be mini-cakes but they pack some serious dessert power.

Applesauce Maraschino Cherry Cake

INGREDIENTS:

2½	cups flour
2	cups sugar
1½	tsp. baking soda
1½	tsp. salt
¼	tsp. baking powder
¼	tsp. cinnamon
½	tsp. cloves
½	tsp. allspice
1½	cups applesauce
½	cup water or Maraschino cherry juice
½	cup shortening
2	eggs
1	cup Maraschino cherries, chopped
½	cup walnuts, finely chopped

1 Preheat oven to 350°.

2 Grease and flour your pan(s). You can use an oblong 13 x 9 x 2 pan or 2-round pans measuring 8-9 inches. Measure all ingredients into a large mixing bowl. Blend for 30 seconds on low speed. Scrape bowl constantly. Beat 3 minutes on high speed. Scrape bowl occasionally.

3 Pour into pan(s). If you make the oblong pan bake for 60-65 minutes at 350°. If you use the round pans bake for 50-55 minutes at 350°. Cool. Frost if desired. ∾

—Susan Lehman of Spokane sends this recipe. It's a cook's dream! You only use one bowl.

Caramel Banana Cake with Walnuts

INGREDIENTS:

1	pkg. yellow or white cake mix
4	eggs
¾	cup water
½	cup cooking oil
1	cup mashed bananas
¾	cup walnuts, chopped
1	pkg. instant butterscotch pudding
	Powdered sugar (optional)

1 In large bowl, combine cake mix, eggs, water, oil, and bananas. Blend until just moistened then beat for two minutes at medium speed. Stir in walnuts.

2 Set aside 1½ cups batter. Stir pudding into remaining mixture until thoroughly blended. Pour into greased and floured 12-cup bundt pan. Top with reserved batter.

3 Bake for 50 minutes at 350°. Cool in pan 10-15 minutes before turning out cake. Sprinkle with powdered sugar if desired. ∾

—Gerry O'Rourke sent in this recipe. The pre-packaged cake mix speeds up your time.

Poppy Seed Cake

INGREDIENTS:

1	pkg. yellow cake mix
4	eggs
1	pkg. instant vanilla pudding (4-servings)
½	cup oil
½	cup sherry
1	cup sour cream or plain yogurt
2	oz. poppy seeds

1 Preheat oven to 350°.

2 Mix all ingredients together. Pour into a greased and floured bundt pan and bake for 45-60 minutes. Let cool for 20 minutes before removing from pan. ❧

—Sue Koutnik of Spokane sends this simple recipe.

Lemon Cake

INGREDIENTS:

Cake:

1	lemon cake mix
2	3 oz. pkgs. lemon Jello
1½	cups hot water
1	12 oz. can lemon-lime soda

Topping:

1	3 oz. box lemon instant pudding mix
1½	cup cold milk
1	6 oz. Cool Whip

1 Bake cake mix as directed.

2 Meanwhile, dissolve lemon jello in 1½ cups hot water. Cool. Then add can of soda.

3 When you pull cake from the oven poke holes in cake with large fork. Pour soda mixture over holes in cake and refrigerate for a few hours.

4 To make topping, beat instant pudding mix with cold milk. Fold in cool whip. Spread over cake and refrigerate. ❧

—June Anderson sent in this recipe from her Spokane kitchen.

Coca-Cola Cake

INGREDIENTS:

Cake:

1	cup coca-cola
½	cup buttermilk
1	cup butter or margarine, softened
1¾	cups sugar
2	large eggs, lightly beaten
2	tsp. vanilla
2	cups flour
¼	cup cocoa
1	tsp. baking soda
1½	cups miniature marshmallows

Frosting:

½	cup butter or margarine
⅓	cup Coca-Cola
3	Tbsp. cocoa
1	16 oz. pkg. powdered sugar
1	Tbsp. vanilla

1 Combine cola and buttermilk; set aside.

2 In a mixing bowl, beat butter at low speed until creamy. Gradually add sugar; beat until well blended. Add egg and vanilla. Beat at low speed until blended.

3 In a separate bowl, combine flour, cocoa, and baking soda. Add dry mixture to butter mixture alternating with cola mixture. Begin and end with flour mixture. Beat at low speed just until blended. Stir in marshmallows.

4 Pour batter into greased and floured 13 x 9 pan. Bake for 30-35 minutes at 350° degrees. Cool for 10 minutes before frosting.

5 While cake is baking you can make the frosting. Bring butter, cola, and cocoa to a boil in a large saucepan over medium heat. Remove from heat; whisk in sugar and vanilla. Pour over warm cake. ❧

—Lois Page of Spokane submitted this recipe for Coca-Cola cake. It may take a little time…but it's well worth the effort!

Quick Fix

Short Cake

With all the fresh berries available in the Northwest during the summer you may want Allie Benzel's recipe for short cake. Benzel is from Ritzville, WA.

❧ Mix 1 cup flour, 2 tsp. baking powder, ½ tsp. salt, ½ cup sugar, 1 egg, ½ cup milk, 2 Tbsp. melted butter and ½ tsp. vanilla. Beat 1 minute. Pour batter into an 8 x 8 baking pan coated with non-stick spray. Bake for 15 minutes at 375°. Top with favorite berries! ❧

Huckleberry Cake

INGREDIENTS:

Batter:

½	cup butter or margarine
¾	cup sugar
2	cups flour
2	tsp. baking powder
½	tsp. salt
1	cup milk

Topping:

5	cups frozen or fresh huckleberries
1½	cups sugar
¾	tsp. cinnamon
1	cup boiling water
2	Tbsp. butter, cut into pieces

1 Preheat oven to 375°.

2 For batter, cream together butter and sugar. In separate bowl, sift together flour, baking powder, and salt. Pour milk into butter mixture and add flour. Mix and beat well. Spread mixture into bottom of greased 9 x 13 or 9 x 14 pan.

3 In a separate bowl, combine sugar, cinnamon and huckleberries. Spread over top of batter. Pour boiling water evenly over all the mixture and dot with butter.

4 Bake for 1 hour. Serve warm or cold. ∾

—Sharon Jarrett sent in this recipe that uses huckleberries. It's hard not to just eat the berries off the bush but if you can wait this recipe is worth it!

Brownstone Cake

INGREDIENTS:

6	Tbsp. cocoa
2	cups sugar
2½	cups flour
2	tsp. baking soda
	pinch of salt
2	cups cream (whipping or sour cream)
4	eggs, well beaten
1	tsp. vanilla

1 Preheat oven to 350°.

2 In a bowl combine, cocoa, sugar, flour, soda, and salt. Add cream, eggs, and vanilla. Once mixture is well-blended pour into 3 greased and floured 9-inch cake pans. Bake for 30-35 minutes. Top with favorite frosting if desired. ∾

—Carol Billing of Republic, WA, sent in this cake recipe. She got it from her mother Mary who received this recipe from a friend in the 1930's.

Apple Pie Cake

INGREDIENTS:

1	cup sugar
¼	cup butter or margarine
1	egg
1	cup flour
½	tsp. nutmeg
1	tsp. baking soda
¼	tsp. salt
1	tsp. cinnamon
2½	cups diced apples
½	cup chopped nuts

1 Preheat oven to 350°.

2 Cream together sugar and butter. Mix with flour, nutmeg, baking soda, salt, cinnamon, apples, and nuts.

3 Pour into greased pie plate. Bake for 45 minutes. ❧

—This combines the best of both worlds, cake and pie! It was sent to us by Bertha Ewell of Spokane.

Apfelkuchen (Apple Cake)

INGREDIENTS:

Cake:

½	cup butter
½	cup sugar
2	eggs
1	Tbsp. vanilla
1½	cups flour
2	tsp. baking powder
3	apples, peeled and thinly sliced
1	tsp. cinnamon

Topping:

⅓	cup sugar
⅔	stick butter
1	cup flour
	Powdered sugar

1 Preheat oven to 350°.

2 In a bowl, combine and mix cake ingredients. Coat spring form pan with butter and flour. Pour ingredients into pan and level.

3 In a separate bowl, combine topping ingredients into a smooth paste. Cover cake with topping mixture. Bake for 45 minutes. Remove from pan when cool. Top with powdered sugar if desired. ❧

—Here's a different version of apple cake. This was sent in by Hilde Schoonover from Spokane.

Pineapple Carrot Cake

INGREDIENTS:

Cake:

2	cups flour
2	tsp. baking soda
1	tsp. baking powder
1	tsp. salt
2	tsp. cinnamon
1¾	cup sugar
1	cup vegetable oil
3	eggs
1	tsp. vanilla
2	cups shredded carrots
1	cup flaked coconut
1	cup walnuts, coarsely chopped
1	8 1/4 oz. can crushed pineapple, drained

Frosting:

1	3 oz. pkg. cream cheese, softened
¼	cup butter, softened
2	cups powdered sugar, sifted
½	tsp. vanilla
2	tsp. milk

1 Preheat oven to 350°.

2 In a large bowl, sift flour, baking soda, baking powder, salt, and cinnamon. Make a well in the center; add in order, sugar, oil, eggs, and vanilla. Beat with a wooden spoon until smooth. Stir in carrots, coconut, walnuts, and pineapple. Blend well. Pour batter into a greased and floured 13 x 9 x 2 baking pan. Bake for 40-45 minutes. (Center should spring back when lightly pressed with fingertip)

3 Cool in pan or on wire rack. Frost.

To make frosting;

Beat cream cheese and butter in medium sized bowl. Beat in sifted powdered sugar. Add vanilla. If necessary, add milk to make consistency desired. ∾

—This recipe may take a little time but it won't take long for it to disappear. It was sent in by Clarkston, WA, resident Flora Edwards.

Rhubarb Cake

June Spencer of Spokane mixes up this easy cake. Perfect for when rhubarb is filling your garden.

§ June dices up four cups of rhubarb and places it into a 13 x 9 glass pan that's sprayed with non-stick coating. She throws in a small package of strawberry jello (dry), 1 cup of sugar, and 1 cup of water. She then sprinkles on a box of white cake mix. She tops the cake mix with 2 Tbsp. of melted butter. She bakes the cake for 40 minutes to an hour at 350°. ∾

Quick Fix

This recipe comes from the kitchen of reporter Erik Loney and his wife Amanda Coulter. Truth be told, Amanda's Grandma created the recipe in a failed attempt to make a lemon meringue pie. Thank goodness for mistakes!

Erik is a field reporter on the KREM 2 team but his most important role is as a husband and father. He and Amanda met while both playing soccer in college (Yep... talented and athletic. We try not to hold it against them). When they are not at work they are at home with their new baby, Cooper. The family of 3 loves playing with their favorite pal, Hunter (a rescued Golden Retriever).

Angel Pie

INGREDIENTS:

Crust:

4	egg whites, yolks reserved
1	tsp. cream of tartar
1	cup sugar
1	tsp. vanilla

Topping:

4	egg yolks
½	cup sugar
1½	lemons (or 1/2 cup lemon juice)
½	pint whipping cream

1 Preheat oven to 300°.

2 For crust: beat egg whites with cream of tartar until stiff and fine grained. Slowly, beat in sugar. Add vanilla. Put into greased pie pan and bake for 1 hour. Cool.

3 For filling: In a saucepan, cook yolks, sugar, and lemon juice over low heat. Stir constantly until thick. Cool. In a separate bowl, whip cream until stiff. Fold in filling.

4 Pour mixture into cooled shell. Refrigerate for at least 2 hours. ❧

—Erik Loney

Bread Pudding

INGREDIENTS:

1	Tbsp. butter
5	slices bread
3	eggs
⅓	cup sugar
2	cups milk, warmed
1	tsp. vanilla
¼	cup raisins
1	tsp. cinnamon
	pinch of salt

1 In a skillet, melt butter. Cube the bread and set pieces into the butter in the skillet.

2 In a separate bowl, beat eggs. Stir in sugar, salt, warmed milk, vanilla, and cinnamon.

3 Sprinkle raisins over bread cubes in the skillet. Pour egg mixture over bread. Cover and cook on low heat for about 20 minutes.

4 Pudding is done when custard is set in the middle. Allow pudding to cool in the skillet before removing. ✎

—This recipe was sent in by Inez Williams of Spokane. It's a perfect treat for the cold winter months. Talk about comfort food!

Mom's Homemade Fudge

INGREDIENTS:

10	graham crackers, finely crushed
3	cups sugar
1-2	Tbsp. cocoa
¼+	tsp. salt
1	tsp. vanilla
1	pkg. mini marshmallows
½	cup peanut butter
1	cup walnuts, chopped (optional)
1½	cups milk

1 In a saucepan, mix sugar, cocoa, and salt. Add milk and bring mixture to a boil at medium heat. Watch closely to prevent scorching. Cook until mixture begins to thicken slightly. (*Whilma tests her mixture by dropping a small spoonful of mixture into a cold cup of water. If the mixture begins to ball-up then it is ready.*)

2 Remove from stovetop. Add vanilla, peanut butter, marshmallows, graham crackers, and walnuts. Mix well and spread into an oiled 9 x 13 pan. Press well and allow to cool before cutting. ✎

—Whilma Clure sent in this recipe from her Rathdrum, ID, kitchen. Perfect for those holiday parties.

Peanut Clusters

INGREDIENTS:

1½	lb. almond bark, white
1	12 oz. package chocolate chips
1	8 oz. pkg. semi-sweet baking chocolate
24-48	oz. dry unsalted peanuts

1 Bertha melts her chocolates in a crock pot set on high. Stirring constantly prevents it from scorching. Add peanuts. Turn off pot.

2 Cover a cookie sheet with waxed paper or foil. Drop small spoonfuls of the mixture onto the covered cookie sheet. Refrigerate until set.

(If you don't have a crock pot then melt chocolate in a double-boiler or heavy saucepan. Watch carefully for scorching.) ∾

—Bertha Ewell sent us this recipe from her Spokane kitchen. Make these at Christmas and you're sure to be the holiday hero.

Buffalo Chips

INGREDIENTS:

1	cup peanut butter
1	cup white Karo syrup
1	cup sugar
4	cups cereal (Wheaties, Corn Flakes, Total or Corn Chex)

1 Set cereal aside in a large mixing bowl.

2 In a saucepan, bring sugar and Karo syrup to a boil. Stir in peanut butter until well blended. Remove mixture from heat.

3 Pour over cereal and mix. Drop by large tablespoons on wax paper. Take dollops of mixture and form into balls. Slightly compress. ∾

—Ilene Greig sent in this recipe with an unusual name. At the time the recipe was created, the family was raising buffalo just West of Spokane. The kids came up with the name for the candy. Believe us, it tastes much better than it sounds!

Lemon Sauce

Stella Derry serves this sauce with a steamed pudding. Stella is from St. Maries, ID.

 § She cooks 1 cup of water, ¾ cup of sugar, 1 rounded tablespoon of cornstarch, and 2 Tbsp. of lemon juice. She cooks it in a pan or microwave until thick. Serve over steamed pudding while warm. ∾

Quick Fix

Fudge Brownies

INGREDIENTS:

¼	cup butter or margarine
1	6 oz. pkg. semi-sweet chocolate chips
1	cup sugar
⅔	cup flour
½	tsp. vanilla
2	eggs
½	cup nuts, chopped (optional)

1 Preheat oven to 375°.

2 In a large bowl, mix together all ingredients. Thoroughly blend for about one minute.

3 Pour mixture into an oiled 8 x 8 pan and bake for 25-30 minutes. Let cool slightly before cutting and serving. ∾

—This recipe was sent in by Jennifer Hancock. Jennifer is from Spokane.

Swedish Date Crumble

INGREDIENTS:

1	lb. dates, chopped
1	cup water
2	cups brown sugar (divided)
1	cup shortening
2	cups flour
2½	cups quick cooking oatmeal
1	tsp. (rounded) baking soda
1	tsp. salt

1 Preheat oven to 350°.

2 In a saucepan, bring dates, one cup brown sugar, and water to a boil. Cook until syrupy consistency.

3 In a separate bowl, mix one cup of brown sugar, shortening, flour, oatmeal, baking soda, and salt. Thoroughly blend until dry and crumbly (*Jack recommends mixing with clean, dry hands*).

4 Firmly press in half of the dry mixture into a well greased 9 x 13 pan. Spread date mixture evenly over the top of dry mixture. Now top the date mixture with the other half of the dry mixture. Pat down firmly. Bake for 30 minutes. Cool on racks and cut into squares. ∾

—Jack Blanchard sent in this recipe from his Coeur d'Alene, ID, kitchen.

Pavlova

INGREDIENTS:

2	egg whites, room temperature
	Pinch of salt
3	Tbsp. water
1	cup sugar
1	tsp. vinegar
1	tsp. vanilla
2	tsp. corn flour
	Whipped cream
	Chocolate shavings

1 Preheat oven to 350°.

2 With a mixer, beat egg whites and pinch of salt until stiff. Add water and sugar while beating slowly. When well-beaten, add vinegar, vanilla, and corn flour.

3 Place well buttered waxed paper on a cookie sheet. Put mixture onto waxed paper creating a circle that is 1-2 inches high. Bake for 5 minutes.

4 Turn off heat and leave tray inside to cook for one more hour. Do not open door. Serve with whipped cream, chocolate shavings and fruit if desired. ✎

—Greg Hughes sent us this dessert that he says was invented in New Zealand (though there is some dispute by Australians!). Greg says it's served at special occasions. We say bake one and it becomes a special occasion.

Fabulous Peach Cobbler

INGREDIENTS:

8	peaches, sliced
1¼	cups sugar, divided
2	Tbsp. lemon juice
½	tsp. almond or vanilla extract
1½	cups flour
1½	tsp. baking powder
2	large eggs, beaten
8	Tbsp. butter, melted
1	Tbsp. brown sugar
½	tsp. cinnamon

1 Preheat oven to 350°.

2 In a bowl, mix peaches, ½ cup sugar, lemon juice, and extract. Transfer mixture to a 2-qt. baking dish. In a separate bowl, mix flour, remaining sugar, baking powder, beaten eggs, and melted butter just until moist (lumps will remain). Do not overmix.

3 Spoon mixture over peaches. Sprinkle with brown sugar and cinnamon. Bake for 35-40 minutes until golden brown. Let cool before serving. ✎

—This recipe was sent in by Evelyn McCartney of Spokane. Perfect for all those freshly picked peaches.

Pumpkin Trifle

INGREDIENTS:	
2	large poppyseed muffins, crumbled
1	16 oz. can pumpkin
1	tsp. cinnamon
¼	tsp. nutmeg
¼	tsp. ginger
⅛	tsp. cloves
4	cups milk, cold
3	3.4 oz. pkgs. instant butterscotch pudding, (sugar-free optional)
1	3.4 oz. pkg. instant vanilla pudding, (sugar-free optional)
2	cups whipping cream

1 Set aside ¼ cup crumbled muffin. Divide remaining crumbs into four portions. Sprinkle one portion into the bottom of a trifle bowl or 3-qt. serving bowl.

2 In a large mixing bowl, combine pumpkin, spices, milk and puddings. Mix until smooth. Spoon half into trifle bowl. Sprinkle with another portion of muffin crumbs.

3 Whip cream until stiff; spoon half into bowl. Top with more muffin crumbs. Top with remaining pumpkin mixture then another portion of crumbs. End the layering with the remaining whipped cream.

4 Cover and chill for at least 2 hours. Top with reserved crumbs and serve. ✎

—This recipe was sent in by Linda Jones. Linda is from Chewelah, WA. She serves this recipe to her family at Thanksgiving. A little switch from the typical pumpkin pie!

Pear Nut Torte

INGREDIENTS:	
1	egg
⅔	cup sugar
½	cup flour
1	tsp. baking powder
¼	tsp. salt
2	large ripe pears, peeled and chopped
½	cup walnuts, chopped
1	tsp. vanilla

1 Preheat oven to 350°.

2 In a mixing bowl, beat egg and sugar until very light. In a separate bowl, mix flour, baking powder, and salt. Stir dry ingredients into egg mixture. Add pears to batter along with nuts and vanilla.

3 Bake in buttered 8 x 8 pan or pie tin for 35 minutes. Serve with whipped topping or ice cream if desired. ✎

—This recipe comes from the Moses Lake, WA, kitchen of Ellie Rysdahl.

www.watrust.com

Washington Trust Bank

IT'S NO SECRET. WE LIVE AND WORK IN A WONDERFUL REGION, BLESSED BY NATURE AND GREATLY ENRICHED BY THE TALENT AND GENIUS OF ITS PEOPLE. AT WASHINGTON TRUST WE'RE PLEASED TO SUPPORT THE CUSTOMERS AND COMMUNITIES WE SERVE.

A SPECIAL
PLACE

PROUD TO BE A SPONSOR OF "KREM 2 IN THE KITCHEN"

For 65 years,

COMMUNITY

has been very important to the owners

and employees of Lawton Printing, Inc.

We take pride in what we do for our

customers and our community.

Congratulations to KREM-TV

for 50 years of contributions

to Spokane.

LAWTONPRINTING

I N C O R P O R A T E D

www.lawtonprinting.com   ■   509.534.1044

Spokane County United Way

All profits from the sale of this book go to the United Way, Spokane County United Way is a locally independent volunteer-driven human care service organization. Through its unique programs, it partners with area volunteers, businesses and non-profit agencies to determine the greatest needs throughout our community and provide services to individuals and families to help them lead a healthier and more independent life.

A special thank you to the following people who helped make this project happen.

BUD BROWN
KREM 2 Vice President & General Manager

RICH LEBENSON
KREM 2 News Director

TAMARA McGREGOR
KREM 2 Dir. of Community Marketing

BARBARA GRANT
KREM 2 Controller

LISA MATHEWS
Lawton Printing

ALAN BISSON
Photographic Designs

COREY HOGAN BIPPES
Sundancer Graphics

www.sundancergraphics.com